THE WORLD OF POETRY

THE WORLD OF POETRY

*Poets and Critics on the Art
and Functions of Poetry*

*Extracts selected and
arranged by*
CLIVE SANSOM

PHOENIX HOUSE
LONDON

Other Books by the Same Author

POETRY

The Cathedral (Methuen)
The Witnesses and Other Poems (Methuen)

VERSE-DRAMA

The World Turned Upside Down (Garnett Miller)

NOVEL

Passion Play (Methuen)

ANTHOLOGIES

By Word of Mouth (Methuen)
The English Heart (Falcon Press)

With Marjorie Gullan
The Poet Speaks (Methuen)

© *Clive Sansom* 1959

Printed in Great Britain
in 11 point Monotype Bembo
by Western Printing Services Ltd for
Phoenix House Ltd, William IV Street
Charing Cross, London WC2

First published 1959

To
RUTH

ACKNOWLEDGMENTS

It would have been impossible to publish this book without the generosity of authors, agents and publishers in allowing so many extracts to be reprinted. The editor would like to record his appreciation of their co-operation.

Every effort has been made to trace owners of other copyright material. Apologies are offered for any material that has been inadvertently included without permission, and acknowledgments will be made in any future edition.

Mr J. Donald Adams for extracts from *The New York Times*.

George Allen & Unwin Ltd for *The Art of the Film* by Ernest Lindgren; and *Scepticism and Poetry* by D. J. James.

Edward Arnold (Publishers) Ltd for *The Discovery of Poetry* by P. H. B. Lyon; and *Tragedy* and *Gifford Lectures* by W. Macneile Dixon.

Lady Cynthia Asquith for an extract from James Barrie.

Mr W. H. Auden for *The Poet's Tongue* (G. Bell & Sons Ltd), extracts from two broadcasts and an introductory essay.

Mrs George Bambridge and A. P. Watt & Son for *Something of Myself* by Rudyard Kipling (Macmillan & Co. Ltd).

Dr Owen Barfield and Faber & Faber Ltd for *Poetic Diction*.

Arthur Barker Ltd for a letter by Stephen Haggard in *The Timeless Quest* by Christopher Hassall.

Mr Clive Bell for an extract from his essays.

Mr Vicars Bell and Faber & Faber Ltd for *On Teaching the English Tongue*.

Blackie & Son Ltd for *On the Teaching of Poetry* by Alexander Haddow.

Geoffrey Bles Ltd for *My Life in Art* by Konstantin Stanislavsky.

Mr Edmund Blunden for lines from his Introduction to *Poems of Many Years* (W. Collins Sons & Co. Ltd).

The Bodley Head Ltd for *Imagination in Dreams* by Frederick Greenwood.

Dr C. L. Boltz and Hamish Hamilton Ltd for *Crown to Mend: A Letter on Poetry*.

Miss Marjorie Boulton and Mr John Johnson for *The Anatomy of Poetry* (Routledge & Kegan Paul Ltd).

Sir Maurice Bowra and Macmillan & Co. Ltd for *The Creative Experiment* and *Inspiration and Poetry*.

The British Council for *English Literature* by B. Ifor Evans.

The British Broadcasting Corporation for extracts from radio talks.

Dr J. Bronowski and the Cambridge University Press for *The Poet's Defence*.

The late Gerald Bullett for *The English Mystics* (Michael Joseph Ltd) and *Readings in English Literature* (A. & C. Black Ltd).

Burns, Oates & Washbourne Ltd for *Prayer and Poetry* by Henri Bremond, translated by Algar Thorold.

Mr Norman Callan and Ernest Benn Ltd for *Poetry in Practice*.

Mrs Campbell for an extract from an article in *The Poetry Review* by the late Roy Campbell.

Mr David Campbell for a review in the *Sydney Bulletin*.

The Syndics of the University Press, Cambridge, for *The Name and Nature of Poetry* by A. E. Housman.

Jonathan Cape Ltd for *The Diaries of Francis Kilvert* edited by William Plomer, and *Shakespeare* and *The Problems of Style* by J. Middleton Murry.

Cassell & Co. Ltd for *The World of Yesterday* by Stefan Zweig, and *The Pursuit of Poetry* by Desmond Flower.

Chapman & Hall Ltd for *Mysticism and Poetry* by A. Allan Brockington.

Chatto & Windus Ltd for *Remembrance of Things Past* by Marcel Proust, translated by C. K. Scott Moncrieff.

Mr John Ciardi for an extract from *The New York Times Book Review*.

Clarendon Press, Oxford, for *An Approach to Shakespeare* by J. W. Mackail.

W. Collins Sons & Co. Ltd. for *From the Unconscious to the Conscious* by Gustav Geley.

Miss Collins and A. P. Watt & Son for extracts from *Chaucer* by G. K. Chesterton (Faber & Faber Ltd).

Constable & Co. Ltd for *The Road to Xanadu* and *Convention and Revolt in Poetry* by J. Livingston Lowes; and *The Brownings* by Osbert Burdett.

Dr David Daiches and Oliver & Boyd Ltd for *The Place of Meaning in Poetry*.

Mrs H. M. Davies and Jonathan Cape Ltd for a short extract by W. H. Davies.

Dr Hugh Sykes Davies for a broadcast talk.

The Literary Trustees of Walter de la Mare, and Faber & Faber Ltd for extracts from a short story, a radio talk, *Desert Islands*, and the prefatory essay to *Behold This Dreamer!*

J. M. Dent & Sons Ltd for *Mozart's Letters* translated by M. M. Bozman; and *The Book of a Naturalist* by W. H. Hudson.

Miss Babette Deutsch for two extracts from *The New York Times Book Review*, and another from *Poetry in Our Time* (Columbia University Press and Geoffrey Cumberlege, Oxford University Press).

Mr James Devaney for *Poetry in Our Time* (Melbourne University Press).

Mr Patric Dickinson for a B.B.C. talk reproduced in *The Listener*.

Miss Elizabeth Drew and the Oxford University Press for *Discovering Poetry*.

Mr Max Eastman for *Enjoyment of Poetry* (Charles Scribner's Sons, New York).

Mr T. S. Eliot for *The Sacred Wood* (Methuen & Co. Ltd); *Selected Essays, Dante, The Four Quartets* and *The Use of Poetry and the Use of Criticism* (Faber & Faber Ltd); *The Music of Poetry* (Jackson Son & Co.); and short extracts from his introductions to other works.

Mr Leonard S. Elton for *A Survey of English Literature* by Oliver Elton.

Professor William Empson and Chatto & Windus Ltd for *Seven Types of Ambiguity*.

Mr A. R. Entwhistle and Thomas Nelson & Sons Ltd for *The Study of Poetry*.

Faber & Faber Ltd and Alfred A. Knopf Inc. for *Poetry and the Age* by Randall Jarrell.

Mr Sean O'Faolain for an extract from *The Short Story* (W. Collins Sons & Co. Ltd).

John Farquharson Ltd, agents for the Henry James Estate, for *The Art of Fiction* by Henry James (Macmillan & Co. Ltd).

Mr Hugh I'Anson Fausset and Jonathan Cape Ltd for *Poets and Pundits*.

Dr Richard Flatter for *Hamlet's Father* (William Heinemann Ltd).

Mr E. M. Forster and Edward Arnold Ltd for *Two Cheers for Democracy*.

M. Max Friedlander and Bruno Cassirer (Publishers) Ltd for *On Art and Connoisseurship*.

Mr Robert Frost, Jonathan Cape Ltd and Henry Holt & Co., for *Complete Poems of Robert Frost*.

Mr Christopher Fry for extracts from *Adam* and other journals.

Professor H. W. Garrod, the Clarendon Press, Oxford, and the Harvard University Press, for *Poetry and the Criticism of Life* and *The Profession of Poetry*.

Mr Stephen Gilbert and Faber & Faber Ltd for *The Milk of Paradise* by Forrest Reid.

Mr Victor Gollancz for *More for Timothy* (V. Gollancz Ltd).

Victor Gollancz Ltd, and Harper & Bros, New York, for *One Man's Meat* by E. B. White.

Mr E. H. Gombrich and Phaidon Press Ltd for *The Story of Art*.

Dr P. Gurrey and the Oxford University Press for *The Appreciation of Poetry*.

Sir George Rostrevor Hamilton and William Heinemann Ltd for *The Tell-Tale Article*.

The Hardy Estate and Macmillan & Co. Ltd. for 'Afterwards' and *The Early Life of Thomas Hardy*.

Dr Rosamond E. M. Harding for *An Anatomy of Inspiration* (Heffer & Sons, Cambridge).

Rupert Hart-Davis Ltd for *Coleridge* by Humphry House.

Dr Erich Heller for *The Hazard of Modern Poetry* (Cambridge University Press).

Mr Ralph Hodgson and Macmillan & Co. Ltd for 'Reason has moons'.

The Hogarth Press, London, and W. W. Norton Co., New York, for *Notebook of Malte Laurids Brigge* by R. M. Rilke, translated by John Linton.

Mr Richard Hughes for a talk on 'The Writer's Duty' in *The Listener*, 22 July 1948.

Mr Aldous Huxley for his essay, 'Vulgarity in Literature'.

Professor J. Isaacs for *The Background to Modern Poetry* (G. Bell & Co.).

Mr Randall Jarrell and A. Knopf Inc. for *Poetry and the Age*.

Mr Charles P. Ker and Macmillan & Co. Ltd for *Form and Style in Poetry* by W. P. Ker.

Mr Alec King and Mr Martin Ketley for *The Control of Language* (Longmans, Green & Co. Ltd, Melbourne).

Professor G. Wilson Knight for *The Wheel of Fire* (Methuen & Co.) and *The Crown of Life* (Oxford University Press).

Sir Stanley Leathes and William Heinemann Ltd for *Rhythm in English Poetry*.

Dr F. R. Leavis and Chatto & Windus Ltd for *New Bearings in English Poetry*.

Mr John Lehmann and Longmans, Green & Co. Ltd for *The Open Night*.

Mr C. Day Lewis and Jonathan Cape Ltd for *An Italian Visit, The Poetic Image* and *Word Over All*.

Mr C. Day Lewis and Mr A. D. Peters for his essay on 'The Nurture of the Imagination', in *Adult Education*, December 1936; *The Colloquial Element in English Poetry* (Literary and Philosophical Society, Newcastle); *Enjoying Poetry* (Cambridge University Press); *The Poet's Task* (Clarendon Press, Oxford); and the broadcast 'Techniques in Poetry' (B.B.C.).

Mr C. Day Lewis and Basil Blackwell Ltd for *A Hope for Poetry* and *Poetry for You*.

Mr F. L. Lucas and The Syndics of the University Press, Cambridge, for *The Decline and Fall of the Romantic Ideal*.

Mr S. R. Lysaght for *A Reading of Poetry* (Macmillan & Co. Ltd).

Macmillan & Co. Ltd, London, for *Oxford Lectures in Poetry* by A. C. Bradley, *The Renaissance* by Walter Pater and the *Selected Letters of Rilke*.

Macmillan & Co., New York, and Mr William Bagley for *The Lesson in Appreciation* by F. H. Hayward.

Mr Louis MacNeice: a broadcast talk.

The executors of the late Thomas Mann, and Martin Secker & Warburg Ltd for extracts from his works.

Methuen & Co. Ltd for short exacts from A. A. Milne and Wyndham Lewis; and the Introduction to *An Anthology of Modern Verse* by Robert Lynd.

Mr Charles Morgan and Macmillan & Co. Ltd for *Reflections in a Mirror* and *Liberties of the Mind*.

The late Gilbert Murray for an extract from 'The Interpretation of Ancient Greek Literature'.

The Editor of the *New York Times Book Review* for permission to use several extracts from articles printed in that journal.

Mr Norman Nicholson for an extract from 'Outposts'.

Oxford University Press for *Reason and Beauty in the Poetic Mind* by Charles Williams; *The Letters of Gerard Manley Hopkins*; *Architecture* by W. R. Lethaby; and *Poetry: Its Music and Meaning* by Lascelles Abercrombie.

Oxford University Press, New York, for *The Achievement of T. S. Eliot* by F. S. Matthieson.

Pearn, Polrlinger & Higham Ltd, and the Estate of the late Mrs Frieda Lawrence fo *The Letters of D. H. Lawrence* (Heinemann Ltd).

Phoenix House Ltd for *On Reading Poetry* by Aubrey de Selincourt.

Professor J. G. Pilley for an essay from *An Outline of Knowledge for Boys and Girls and their Parents* (Victor Gollancz Ltd).

Sir Isaac Pitman & Sons for *Poetry as a Representative Art* by G. L. Raymond.

The late Arthur Quiller Couch for an essay on 'Poetry' whose publishers we have been unable to trace.

Sir Herbert Read and Faber & Faber Ltd for *Collected Essays in Literary Criticism*.

Professor I. A. Richards and Routledge & Kegan Paul Ltd for *Science and Poetry*, *Practical Criticism*, and *Principles of Literary Criticism*.

Mrs Janet Roberts for *A Critique of Poetry* by Michael Roberts (Faber & Faber Ltd).

Mr W. R. Rodgers for an extract from a B.B.C. broadcast.

Mr Alan Rook for an article in *The Poetry Review*.

Routledge & Kegan Paul Ltd for *Speculations* by T. E. Hulme, and the works of C. J. Jung.

Mr Diarmuid Russell and Macmillan & Co. Ltd for *The Living Torch* by 'A.E.' (G. W. Russell).

Mr Siegfried Sassoon for essay, 'On Poetry'.

Martin Secker & Warburg Ltd for *The Culture of Cities* by Lewis Mumford.

Messrs Shakespear & Parkyn and the Committee for Ezra Pound for six extracts from his works.

Sheed & Ward Ltd for *The Spiritual Letters of Dom John Chapman*.

Sidgwick & Johnson Ltd for *Letters to a Young Poet* by R. M. Rilke, translated by Reginald Snell; and for an extract from a letter by Rupert Brooke quoted in his *Collected Poems*.

Sir Osbert Sitwell for *A Letter to My Son* (Duckworth & Co. Ltd).

South Place Ethical Society for extracts from the Conway Memorial Lecture for 1923: *The Poet and Communication* by John Drinkwater, subsequently published by C. A. Watts & Co. Ltd.

Mr Stephen Spender for *Life and the Poet* (Secker and Warburg Ltd); and *The Making of a Poem* and *World within World* (Hamish Hamilton Ltd).

M. Georges Superveille for extracts from a broadcast talk in *The Listener*, 12 June 1952.

The late Arthur Symons for extracts from *The Romantic Movement in English Poetry* (Constable & Co.).

The Lord Tennyson and his Trustees for quotations from the writings of his grandfather and great-grandfather.

Mr E. M. W. Tillyard and Chatto & Windus Ltd for *Poetry Direct and Oblique*.

The Editor of *The Times Literary Supplement* for short extracts of reviews and articles which first appeared in that journal.

Mr E. W. F. Tomlin for extracts from lectures delivered for the Speech Fellowship.

Mr Keith Vaughan for a quotation from *Penguin New Writing*.

Miss R. Walsh for part of a letter in *The Listener*.

Mr Rex Warner for extracts from *Penguin New Writing* and a broadcast talk.

Mr George Whalley and Routledge & Kegan Paul Ltd for *Poetic Process*.

Mr John Wheelock and Charles Scribner's Sons, New York, for *Poets of Today*.

Mr Richard Wilbur for *The Genie and the Bottle* (Twayne Publishing Co., New York).

Professor Basil Willey for a broadcast talk in *The Listener*.

Miss Margaret Willy and the English Association for an article in *English*.

Professor J. Dover Wilson and The Syndics of the Cambridge University Press for *The Essential Shakespeare*.

Dr K. M. Wilson and Jonathan Cape Ltd for *Sound and Meaning in English Poetry*.

Miss Irene Willis and the Trustees of the late Mrs Hardy's Estate for extracts from the Notebooks of Thomas Hardy.

Professor Leonard Woolf and the Hogarth Press for *Letter to a Young Poet* by Virginia Woolf.

Mr R. H. Ward for an article in *The Aryan Path*.

Mrs Yeats and Messrs A. P. Watt & Son for 'A Prayer for Old Age', and *Autobiographies* by W. B. Yeats (Macmillan & Co. Ltd).

I am also indebted to the Buxton Forman edition (Oxford University Press) for extracts from the letters of John Keats.

CONTENTS

FOREWORD

This anthology has gradually compiled itself over the last twenty-five years. And, to a large extent, it has arranged itself. Only in the last six months, since publication was considered, have I taken a conscious hand in shaping it, removing superfluous fat in one place and building up in another where it seemed unduly lean. But a subconscious design appears to have been behind it from the start, and the book does present—I won't say a philosophy of poetry: that is too grandiloquent a term—but perhaps a theory of poetry. Not my theory, but a composite one based on the writings of many critics and particularly those who have also been poets.

That is why each passage needs to be read as part of the section in which it finds itself; because there are sometimes two divergent opinions, and the truth comes, it seems to me, in a balance between them. Similarly, each section is seen in better perspective against the other sections, and there is, through the book, a logical or at least a poetic sequence.

I wish to thank those authors, agents and publishers who have so kindly contributed to this bran-tub of commentary; and to apologize for interpolating my own views where it seemed necessary to provide a linking passage or a judicial summing-up. At least these are separated from their more distinguished companions.

I hope that the book will prove useful to students and general readers, leading them not only to the authors with whose words I have played jackdaw, but to poetry itself. The world was never more in need of the special kind of sight that poetry can give, and its special kind of truth.

C.S.

THE PLACE OF POETRY

I know that poetry is indispensable,
but I do not know for what.
JEAN COCTEAU

It . . . purges from our inward sight the film of familiarity which obscures from us the wonder of our being. It compels us to feel that which we perceive, and to imagine that which we know.

P. B. SHELLEY: *A Defence of Poetry*, 1820

What makes me so sure that poetry is the greatest of the literary arts? I think this is so because nothing in man's experience of communication through language has moved him so deeply, has sustained him so surely in his hours of confusion and despair, has made him so deeply and intensely aware of beauty and the joy of being alive.

J. DONALD ADAMS: *New York Times Book Review*

Poetry is not assumed by man as he puts on a ceremonial dress. It is the outcrop of a movement and harmony in his nature, a true response to a true cause. The degree to which we find ourselves foreign to it is the degree to which we have separated ourselves from instinctive knowledge; the degree to which we have accepted ourselves and the world at their face value.

CHRISTOPHER FRY: 'Return of a Prodigal', *Vogue*, U.S.A.

It enables him to escape out of the make-believe existence of everyday in which perhaps an employer seems more huge and imminent than God, and to explore reality, where God and love and beauty and life and death are seen in truer proportions, and where the desire of the heart is at least brought within sight of a goal.

ROBERT LYND: 'On Poetry and the Modern Man', 1921

B

Burdened with the complexity of the lives we lead, fretting over appearances, netted in with anxieties and apprehensions, half smothered in drifts of tepid thoughts and tepid feelings, we may refuse what poetry has to give; but under its influence serenity returns to the troubled mind, the world crumbles, loveliness shines like flowers after rain, and the further reality is once more charged with mystery.

WALTER DE LA MARE: 'Dream and Imagination',
Behold This Dreamer, 1939

Poetry cannot cure cancer, nor put an end to fire, famine, and flood. But it can provide a fusion of relaxation and excitement without the penalties attaching to either. To a greater degree than the other arts, it can reveal the conditions of living. This should help us to amend them.

BABETTE DEUTSCH: *Poetry in Our Time*, 1956

The effect of poetry . . . on the lives of men will always be a subject of controversy, as it cannot ever be as directly apparent as the effect of an electric turbine on the lights of a town; but nevertheless I am convinced that as Newton's discoveries completely changed man's outlook in the physical world, and Einstein's discoveries are again changing that outlook today, so the work of the great poets has, in a far more profound and spiritual sense, completely conditioned the whole attitude to life and death, their value and their meaning, of the culture in whose veins their work like life-blood runs. Poetry works so secretly and so insensibly for the most part, that one cannot trace with anything approaching scientific satisfaction the tracks it makes, the flowers that burst into blossom in its path, but I will assert that as the great richness and vitality of English poetry for three hundred and fifty years is inconceivable without Shakespeare, so the course of English history, the English civilization we have inherited, is inconceivable without that poetry. . . . Poets, one might say, are the lobes of balance we cannot do without in times of violent transformation and uncertainty, when old creeds are broken up and new false creeds, eagerly grasped, are leading men into their hidden traps of despair.

JOHN LEHMANN: 'The Poet in the Modern World',
The Open Night, 1952

The cultivation of poetry is never more to be desired than at periods when, from an excess of the selfish and calculating principle, the accumulation of the materials of external life exceed the quantity of the power of assimilating them to the internal laws of human nature.

P. B. SHELLEY: *A Defence of Poetry*, 1820

It is arguable that mechanical inventions, with their social effects, and a too sudden diffusion of indigestible ideas, are disturbing throughout the world the whole order of human mentality, that our minds are, as it were, becoming of an inferior shape—thin, brittle and patchy, rather than controllable and coherent. It is possible that the burden of information and consciousness that a growing mind has now to carry may be too much for its natural strength. If it is not too much already, it may soon become so, for the situation is likely to grow worse before it is better. Therefore, if there be any means by which we may artificially strengthen our minds' capacity to order themselves, we must avail ourselves of them. And of all possible means, Poetry, the unique linguistic instrument by which our minds have ordered their thoughts, emotions, desires . . . in the past, seems to be the most serviceable. It may well be a matter of some urgency to us, in the interests of our standard of civilization, to make this highest form of language more accessible. From the beginning, civilization has been dependent upon speech, for words are our chief link with the past and with one another, and the channel of our spiritual inheritance.

I. A. RICHARDS: *Practical Criticism*, 1929

The people which ceases to care for its literary inheritance becomes barbaric; the people which ceases to produce literature ceases to move in thought and sensibility. The poetry of a people takes its life from the people's speech and in turn gives life to it; and represents its highest point of consciousness, its greatest power and its most delicate sensibility.

T.S. ELIOT: Introduction to *The Use of Poetry and the Use of Criticism*, 1933

Art is valuable not because it is educational (though it may be), not because it is recreative (though it may be), not because everyone enjoys it (for everyone does not), not even because it has to do with beauty. It is valuable because it has to do with order, and creates little worlds of its own, possessing internal harmony in the bosom of this disordered planet. It is needed at once and now . . . It is the activity which brought man out of original darkness and differentiates him from the beasts, and we must continue to practise and respect it through the darkness of today.

E. M. FORSTER: 'The Challenge of Our Time' in
Two Cheers for Democracy, 1946

Rilke tells a story in which it is the sea and the distance that becomes the image of the poet's reality. A rowing-boat sets out on a difficult passage. The oarsmen labour in exact rhythm. There is no sign yet of the destination. Suddenly a man, seemingly idle, breaks out into song. And if the labour of the oarsmen meaninglessly defeats the real resistance of the real waves, it is the idle singer who magically conquers the despair of apparent aimlessness. While the people next to him try to come to grips with the element that is next to them, his voice seems to bind the boat to the farthest distance so that the farthest distance draws it towards itself. 'I don't know why and how', is Rilke's conclusion, 'but suddenly I understood the situation of the poet, his place and function in this age.'

ERICH HELLER: *The Hazard of Modern Poetry*, 1953

❧ DEFINITIONS ❧

*'What is poetry?'—a question as impossible to
answer as Pilate's 'What is truth?'*

C. DAY LEWIS

This, however, has not deterred poets from making the attempt, and the following is a selection of their answers. Each, in finding one facet of the truth, has overlooked a dozen others; but between them they present, if not a definition of poetry, at least some 'Notes towards a definition'.

   ⊛   ⊛   ⊛

Poetry is the spontaneous overflow of powerful feelings . . .

WILLIAM WORDSWORTH

Poetry, in a general sense, may be defined to be 'the expression of the imagination'.

P. B. SHELLEY

Poetry is the language of the imagination and the passions.

WILLIAM HAZLITT

Poetry is imaginative passion.

LEIGH HUNT

Poetry is the best words in the best order.

S. T. COLERIDGE: *Table Talk*

An English poet once declared that poetry is the best words in the best order—the sort of thing that makes the critics of less inhibited nations wonder how the English ever contrive to write poetry at all. . . .

C. DAY LEWIS: *The Colloquial Element in English Poetry*, 1947

The definition of good prose is—proper words in their proper places; of good poetry—the most proper words in their proper places.

S. T. COLERIDGE: *Table Talk*, 3 July 1833

When Coleridge made this assertion his *mind* was not in its proper place.

FRANK SWINNERTON[1]

Poetry may be defined as a way of remembering what it would impoverish us to forget.

ROBERT FROST

A concise and simple way of saying great things.

EDWARD FITZGERALD

Poetry is emotion put into measure.

THOMAS HARDY

Perfection of form united with a significance of feeling.

T. S. ELIOT

Memorable speech.

W. H. AUDEN

Poetry is nothing less than the most perfect speech of man, that in which he comes nearest to being able to utter the truth.

MATTHEW ARNOLD: *Essays in Criticism*, 1888

Poetry is a form of speech for the better expression of emotional ideas.

HERBERT SPENCER: Essay, 'Origin and Function of Music'

Poetry is a precision instrument for recording a man's reactions to life.

LOUIS MACNEICE

---

[1] But Coleridge's mind, which had a habit of wandering between the sublime and the ridiculous, makes many journeys to sublimity in the chapters that follow.

Poetry is the criticism of life.

MATTHEW ARNOLD

What a dismal definition!—that poetry should be critical of anything! Is it not rather life itself that is the final criticism of poetry?

F. L. LUCAS

Poetry . . . is the attempt to imagine, in terms of the transitory forms of the present in which a generation lives, the universal nature of man's being.

STEPHEN SPENDER

Poetry is the expression of the emotion caused by an intense realization of life.

S. R. LYSAGHT

Poetry is the language in which man explores his own amazement.

CHRISTOPHER FRY

Poetry is . . . a way of using words to say things which could not possibly be said in any other way, things which in a sense do not *exist* till they are born (or re-born) in poetry.

C. DAY LEWIS

Wherever a movement of imagination or passion is impressed on the mind, by which it seeks to prolong and repeat the emotion, to bring all other objects into accord with it, and to give the same movement of harmony, sustained and continuous, or gradually varied according to the occasion, to the sounds that express it—this is poetry.

WILLIAM HAZLITT: Lectures on the English Poets, 1818

Many definitions have been attempted, but a satisfactory one has never been found. For they . . . are necessarily subjective and reveal only an individual aspect of the truth. The definitions produced by poets themselves naturally are framed to suit their own poetry, but on a more universal application their weakness is revealed.

FORREST REID: The Milk of Paradise, 1946

BOSWELL: 'Then, sir, what is poetry?'
JOHNSON: 'Why, sir, it is much easier to say what it is not. We all *know* what light is, but it is not easy to *tell* what it is.'

We then talked of the aesthetic writers, who labour to express the nature of poetry and the poet in abstract definitions, without arriving at any clear result. 'What need of much definition?' said Goethe. 'Lively feeling of situations, and power to express them, make the poet.'

Conversations with Eckermann, 11 June 1825

*   *   *

You pays your money and you takes your choice. Here, to end this section is my own contribution:

Poetry is a rhythmical form of words which expresses an imaginative-emotional-intellectual experience of the writer's, and expresses it in such a way that it creates a similar experience in the mind of his reader or listener.

But this is not satisfactory either, because prose can sometimes do as much. Poetry is too elusive to be caught in any convenient net of words. We find it, if we find it at all, by divination, rather than definition. Perhaps, after all, the most successful attempt was the schoolboy's: 'Poetry is the stuff that poets write.'

❧ THE POET ❧

The Cliff of Poesy towers above me. I am one
that 'gathers Samphire, dreadful trade'.[1]
JOHN KEATS

Some, whose temper of body humours the constitution of their souls,
are born poets; though indeed all are naturally inclined into rhythm.

THOMAS BROWNE: *Religio Medici*, 1642

Just . . . as the leopard or the lamb is one species of living creature, and
the hawk or the ox is another, so among humans stands out this particular temperament. It shares the life that is common to all men, but
it possesses life in this kind more acutely and abundantly, and it has
the faculty of communicating it. Why this is, and why it is the gift
in particular of certain races, who can say?

WALTER DE LA MARE: 'Dream and Imagination',
Behold This Dreamer, 1939

What is a Poet? He is a man speaking to men: a man, it is true, endowed with more lively sensibility, more enthusiasm and tenderness,
who has a greater knowledge of human nature, and a more comprehensive soul, than are supposed to be common among mankind;
a man pleased with his own passions and volitions, and who rejoices
more than other men in the spirit of life that is in him; delighting to
contemplate similar volitions and passions as manifested in the goings-
on of the Universe, and habitually impelled to create them where he
does not find them.

WILLIAM WORDSWORTH: Preface to second edition of
Lyrical Ballads, 1800

⊛　　⊛　　⊛

This worthier-than-thou conception of the poet must be one reason
why the average man looks askance at him. And is it true? Is the poet

[1] *King Lear*, Act IV, Sc. 6.

necessarily endowed with a more lively sensibility than his neighbour, more enthusiasm and tenderness? I doubt it. I have known many people more sensitive than myself, more aware of beauty, more kindly and enthusiastic, but they have not written poetry. It is only in this respect that I am superior to them.

Isn't it rather that a poet is a peculiar piece of mechanism which has its sensitiveness and emotions geared to language? One man may feel something deeply; his whole being is affected by it, but he remains silent. Another, in the same situation, may feel less deeply in the human sense—his attitude may even seem strangely remote and impersonal—but it finds expression in poetry. Indeed one might say that the essential difference between the poet and other men is not that he feels more deeply, but that he feels more deeply and consistently in words. However, we must let Wordsworth continue. . . .

⊛   ⊛   ⊛

He is retired as noontide dew,
Or fountain in a noon-day grove;
And you must love him, ere to you
He will seem worthy of your love.

The outward shows of sky and earth,
Of hill and valley, he has viewed;
And impulses of deeper birth
Have come to him in solitude.

In common things that round us lie,
Some random truths he can impart—
The harvest of a quiet eye
That broods and sleeps on his own heart.

WILLIAM WORDSWORTH: From 'A Poet's Epitaph', 1799

There are three requisites to form the poet: 1. Sensibility; 2. Imagination; 3. Power of Association.

S. T. COLERIDGE: 4th Lecture on Shakespeare, 1811–12

The poet, then, must feel in images: he must grasp the connections between things—but grasp them emotionally, rather than logically, and he must be capable of seeing one thing in terms of another. Now if we consider those three abilities, we realize that there is a certain innocence, a child-like nature common to all of them. Imagination demands—and not only from the poet—a quality of innocence.

C. DAY LEWIS: 'The Nurture of the Imagination', 1936

Compared with him, the ordinary man suppresses nine-tenths of his impulses, because he is incapable of managing them without confusion. He goes about in blinkers because what he would otherwise see would upset him. But the poet through his superior power of ordering experience is freed from this necessity. Impulses which commonly interfere with one another and are conflicting, independent, and mutually destructive, in him combine into a stable poise. He selects, of course, but the range of suppression which is necessary for him is diminished, and for this very reason such suppressions as he makes are more vigorously carried out. Hence the curious local callousness of the artist which so often strikes the observer.

I. A. RICHARDS: *Principles of Literary Criticism*, 1924

A being, like all the rest of mankind, on a planet swarming with his fellow creatures, teaming with life, thronged with hordes and herds of his brothers, and yet a being living in an indestructible loneliness. . . . A being essentially inexplicable and inexpressible, yet struggling passionately to express and explain himself, to convey the unique quality of his human consciousness, of his traffic with the worlds of brain and blood.

ELIZABETH DREW: *Discovering Poetry*, 1933

To be a poet is to apprehend the true and the beautiful; in a word, the good which exists in the relation subsisting, first between existence and perception, and secondly between perception and expression.

P. B. SHELLEY: *A Defence of Poetry*, 1820

He is a point of intensest feeling thrown out like an antenna by the social body to test the amorphous limits of existence, the nature of 'becoming'. He is the advance-guard of experience.

HERBERT READ

The poet is a man who, seeing something ineffable behind the things of this world, and seeing it as beauty, makes an effort to express it in words: in words that, even as they come, make the vision itself a little clearer to himself and to others.

VICTOR GOLLANCZ: *More for Timothy*, 1953

❋   ❋   ❋

If the safest definition of poetry was 'The stuff that poets write', the most satisfactory description of the poet would be, 'A man who writes poetry'. But perhaps, through the foregoing paragraphs, a composite portrait emerges which makes a bolder attempt at likeness. Now comes the question: What is the special quality that makes a poet—what sets the dynamo running?

❧ IMAGINATION ❧

. . . what Nature gave me at my birth,
My shaping spirit of Imagination.
WILLIAM WORDSWORTH

That intellectual lens through the medium of which the poetical observer *sees* the objects of his observation, modified both in form and colour.

WILLIAM WORDSWORTH

One Power alone makes a Poet: Imagination, the Divine Vision.

WILLIAM BLAKE: annotations to Wordsworth's poems

Imagination is to space what memory is to time—a faculty that presents to the mind data which are not immediately present to the senses.

C. DAY LEWIS: 'The Nurture of the Imagination', 1936

Imaginatio means: 1. the impression made by a phenomenon, as by a seal on wax; 2. the reconstruction, in the memory, of such an impression; 3. the construction, from past impressions, of some new image.

F. L. LUCAS: *Decline and Fall of the Romantic Ideal*, 1936

The poet's imagination is almost exactly the opposite of everything we mean by the will: it feeds on contemplation, when the will feeds on action; it is primarily a passive quality, a more or less trained sensitiveness, the matrix on which nature breeds art; it must be a re-agent before it can become an agent. Yet the poetic word, imagination's child, when it is made flesh, can be one of the most powerful agents in the world. . . .

C. DAY LEWIS: 'The Nurture of the Imagination'

The incalculable power which we call Imagination, whose goal is the unfathomable something we name Beauty, is no alien visitant, but an agency which operates through faculties of universal exercise upon that streaming chaos of impressions through which we hourly move. . . . One office of the imagination is to curb and rudder the clustering associations which throng up from the nether depths of consciousness, until out of the thick of the huddle springs beauty.

JOHN LIVINGSTON LOWES: *The Road to Xanadu*, 1930

Imagination, which is Spiritual Sensation.

WILLIAM BLAKE

'Sensation', of this kind, involves the whole being of man; it is physical, emotional, intellectual, spiritual, all at the same time, and these indistinguishably. And it is precisely this fourfold unity that Blake discerned and asserted when he described Imagination as the Fourfold Human 'Sensation', in the sense in which Keats used it, ['O for a life of Sensations rather than of Thoughts'], and in which we have used it here, is always 'spiritual', as Blake meant the word. The almost imperceptible distinction between Keats' use and Blake's is apparent in Keats' sentence: 'The Genius of Poetry must work out its own salvation in a man; it cannot be matured by law and precept, but by sensation and watchfulness in itself. That which is creative must create itself.' The words touch the very core of Shakespeare's genius, and through Keats serve to link Shakespeare and Blake together. 'Sensation and watchfulness in itself'—a total experience suffused by awareness—is, I believe, what Blake meant by 'spiritual sensation'; and it is as near as we shall get to a definition of Imagination—the means and instrument by which, in man, that which is creative creates itself.

J. MIDDLETON MURRY: *Shakespeare*, 1936

The Imagination may be compared to Adam's dream—he awoke and found it truth.

JOHN KEATS in a letter to Benjamin Bailey, 22 November 1817

The whole visible universe is but an array of images and signs to which the imagination gives a place and a relative value; it is a sort of fodder which the imagination must digest and transform. All the faculties of

man's soul must be subordinated to the imagination, which can call
upon them all at once.

CHARLES BAUDELAIRE

Douglas Cooper, discussing Baudelaire's ideas in *The Listener*, adds:
'Imagination is a scientific faculty which understands universal analogies,
or what mystical religion calls "correspondencies".'

❊   ❊   ❊

Imagination, that fuses the familiar and the strange, the thing I feel
and the thing I see, the world within and the world without, into a
tertium quid that interprets both.

JOHN LIVINGSTON LOWES: *Convention and Revolt in Poetry*, 1919

I conceive it as the habit, innate but capable of cultivation, of feeling
emotion in images. It is the faculty which grasps those invisible links
that bind together the visible points of existence—a faculty of vision.

C. DAY LEWIS: 'The Nurture of the Imagination', 1936

Imagination . . . the power by which one image or feeling is made to
modify many others, and by a sort of fusion to force many into one;
that which afterwards showed itself in such might and energy in *Lear*,
where the deep anguish of a father spreads the feeling of ingratitude
and cruelty over the very elements of heaven;—and which, combining
many circumstances into one moment of consciousness, tends to produce that ultimate end of all human thought and human feeling,
unity . . .

S. T. COLERIDGE: *Biographia Literaria*, 1817

The poet, described in ideal perfection, brings the whole soul of man
into activity, with the subordination of its faculties to each other
according to their relative worth and dignity. He diffuses a tone and
spirit of unity, that blends and (as it were) *fuses*, each into each, by
that synthetic and magical power, to which I would exclusively
appropriate the name of Imagination. This power, first put in action
by the will and understanding, and retained under their irremissive,
though gentle and unnoticed control . . . reveals itself in the balance or
reconcilement of opposite or discordant qualities: of sameness, with

difference; of the general with the concrete; the idea with the image; the individual with the representative; the sense of novelty and freshness with old and familiar objects; a more than usual state of emotion with more than usual order; judgment ever awake and steady self-possession, with enthusiasm and feeling profound or vehement; and while it blends and harmonizes the natural and the artificial, still subordinates art to nature; the manner to the matter; and our admiration of the poet to our sympathy with the poetry.

s. t. coleridge: *Biographia Literaria*, 1817

Imagination modifies images, and gives unity to variety; it sees all things in one.

s. t. coleridge: *Table Talk*, 23 June 1834

'The imagination', said Coleridge once, recalling a noble phrase from Jeremy Taylor's *Via Pacis*, 'sees all things in one.' It sees the Free Life— the endless flux of the unfathomed sea of facts and images—but it sees also the controlling Form. And when it acts on what it sees, through the long patience of the will, the flux itself is transformed and fixed in the clarity of a realized design. For there enter into the imaginative creation three factors which reciprocally interplay; the Well, and the Vision, and the Will. Without the Vision, the chaos of elements remains a chaos, and the Form sleeps forever in the vast chambers of unborn designs. Yet in *that* chaos only could creative Vision ever see *this* Form. Nor without the co-operant Will, obedient to the Vision, may the pattern perceived in the huddle attain objective reality. Yet manifold though the ways of the creative faculty may be, the upshot is one: from the empire of chaos a new tract of cosmos has been retrieved. . . .

john livingston lowes: *The Road to Xanadu*, 1930

❧ THOUGHT AND FEELING ❧

God guard me from those thoughts men think
In the mind alone;
He that sings a lasting song
Thinks in a marrow-bone.
W. B. YEATS, 'A Prayer for Old Age', *Collected Poems*

He [Yeats] was not a man of intellect, but, for a poet, he was something better, a man of great intellectual passion.

SEAN O'FAOLAIN in *The Sunday Times*

In an intensely civilized period like our own, it may only be possible to imagine by *thinking away* ordinary ideas: in other words, by thinking away thought. Therefore it is not paradoxical that the two finest poets of the present day—T. S. Eliot and W. B. Yeats—are both men of outstanding intellect.

E. W. F. TOMLIN: Lectures on Modern Poetry, 1936

⊛   ⊛   ⊛

One of the great obstacles to the understanding of poetry is its simplicity. Although it is often looked upon as a sophisticated development, it also connects with the primitive beginnings of language. It belongs to childhood and to the childhood of the race. It is the Alpha and the Omega of speech. The average reader—whose brain has been educated in analysis, calculation and reasoning, and whose heart and imagination are left almost illiterate—looks at poetry as if it were the words of a textbook. Examinations, and the kind of mind encouraged by examinations, have excised his intellect so that it exists by itself, like an organ preserved in a jar of formalin. He dissects a poem for its 'thoughts', forgetting that poetry thinks with its nerves. We cannot know how its brain is functioning until we've felt its pulse.

⊛   ⊛   ⊛

True art cannot exist without emotion.

J. W. GOETHE in letter to Müller, 1808

C

If we are not moved, then it is, as poetry, meaningless.

T. S. ELIOT

The Poet takes note of nothing that he cannot feel emotionally.

THOMAS HARDY: Notes quoted in *The Early Life of Thomas Hardy*

It is not enough for an author to see a thing with his eyes; he must apprehend it with his nerves, his heart, his bowels.

W. SOMERSET MAUGHAM

What every poet starts from is his own emotions.

T. S. ELIOT

When a man is moved in the first place to write a poem, or to create in any other art, it is his feelings which impel him, not reason.

JAMES DEVANEY: *Poetry in Our Time*, 1952

All lyrical poetry beats with the heart, tells not of things coldly and calmly considered, but of things seen and felt in a sudden clearness of the senses, and with a flame in the thought.

WALTER DE LA MARE: *Behold This Dreamer*, 1939

When we study poetry intellectually, we must think of its effect on us and try to account for it; but we should not forget that if the poem is a good one the poet probably wrote it under the stimulus of some over-whelmingly powerful emotional urge, and some of the poet's emotion may be passed on to us by processes that are not conscious. Poetry is more akin to magic, prayer, prophecy and myth than to knitting or fretwork; to look at it purely from the formally technical point of view and never surrender to it, is as misleading as to wallow all the time in indefinable emotion about it.

MARJORIE BOULTON: *The Anatomy of Poetry*, 1953

It is essential to poetry . . . that it be impassioned, and be able to move our feelings and awaken our affections.

S. T. COLERIDGE: *Biographia Literaria*, 1817

What comes from the heart goes to the heart.

s. t. coleridge in table-talk recorded by Samuel Rogers

Thought by itself makes no poet at all. Feeling, even destitute of conscious thought, stands a far better poetical chance, being a sort of thought without the process of thinking—a grasper of the truth without seeing it.

LEIGH HUNT

. . . not to transmit thought but to set up in the reader's sense a vibration corresponding to what was felt by the writer—is the peculiar function of poetry.

a. e. housman: *The Name and Nature of Poetry*, 1933

. . . Poems and stories are written by memory and desire, love and hatred, daydreams and nightmares—by a being, not a brain.

randall jarrell: *Poetry and the Age*, 1955

. . . the third condition, passion, provides that neither thought nor imagery shall be simply objective, but that the *passio vera* of humanity shall warm and animate both.

s. t. coleridge: Lectures on Poetry, 1818

Sense-impressions being the material of his art, it is along the pulse of feeling that these are carried into the poet's heart, and rooted there, to bloom perhaps into imagery in due season. A pure intelligence could not be a poet. A poet's thoughts are steeped in feeling.

j. c. smith: *A Study of Wordsworth*, 1944

Language has two main functions, the control of ideas and the control of emotions. . . . Pig-headed literalmindness in the reading of poetry and emotional interpretation of scientific statements are common failings of those who cannot distinguish between the two uses of words.

michael roberts: *A Critique of Poetry*, 1934

It is the inclusion of feeling that makes the difference between poetry and science. Science is not concerned merely with analysing things:

it also must try to relate them with each other and thus discover the natural laws at work behind them. But the scientist uses theory, observation and experiment to relate his facts with each other, whereas the poet uses his own feelings, his emotions. It would be all wrong for a scientist to get emotional when he describes a daffodil; and it would be all wrong for a poet *not* to.

C. DAY LEWIS: *Poetry for You*, 1944

Misunderstanding and under-estimation of poetry is mainly due to over-insistence on the thought in separation from the rest. We can see still more clearly that thought is not the prime factor if we consider for a moment not the experience of the reader but that of the poet. Why does the poet use these words and no others? Not because they stand for a series of thoughts which in themselves are what he is concerned to communicate. It is never what a poem *says* which matters, but what it *is*. The poet is not writing as a scientist. He uses these words because the interests whose movement is the growth of the poem combine to bring them, just in this form, into his consciousness *as a means of ordering, controlling and consolidating* the uttered experience of which they are themselves a main part. The experience itself, the tide of impulses sweeping through the mind, is the source and the sanction of the words.

I. A. RICHARDS: *Science and Poetry*, 1935

Poetic language is an incarnation, not a transcription of thought: it is a seizing on truth beyond the writer's personal thinking through submission to the object. Such submission conditions the deepest self-realization, since what normally passes for thought is merely a cheap currency drawn from and touching the mental centres only. . . .

G. WILSON KNIGHT: *The Crown of Life*, 1948

✺ FEELING AND THOUGHT ✺

*The poet cannot think too deeply, if he thinks
through the imagination.*
JOHN LIVINGSTON LOWES

Poetry cannot be reached by the 'mental centres' alone. But neither can the best of it be reached by the emotions alone—only by the operation of the two together, the two working as one. The curse of education is that it so often uncouples them. It has been said that poetry belongs to childhood, and it is true in this: that in a small child thought has not yet been separated from feeling. His brain works through his heart; his heart sets off the brain. All children, at some time in their development, are unconscious poets. And it is only by becoming as little children—rejecting neither thought nor feeling, but allowing them to be blended by the imagination—that we can enter the kingdom of poetry.

        ⊛   ⊛   ⊛

. . . All good poetry is the spontaneous overflow of powerful feelings; and though this be true, poems to which any value can be attached were never produced on any variety of subjects but by a man who, being possessed of more than usual organic sensibility, had also thought long and deeply.

WILLIAM WORDSWORTH: Preface to *Lyrical Ballads*,
Third Edition, 1802

It will be obvious that poetry is emotive language; but it is unwise to consider it as a kind of language designed to rouse only, or chiefly, our emotions. The meaning that the devices of poetry may pack into language is not only emotive meaning, but *all* the meaning that the words are capable of suggesting, referential as well as emotive. . . . The poet writes with the whole of himself, with the whole range of his personality, with all his faculties at work, with an intelligence that is warmed by feeling, and with feeling illuminated by intelligence.

ALEC KING and MARTIN KETLEY: *The Control of Language*, 1939

They say that we can create poetry out of words chosen entirely for their beautiful sound and vague emotional suggestions. Some have even maintained that the poet ignores the intellectual meaning of words. Now it would seem, *prima facie*, a silly thing for a poet to throw overboard an element in his medium which contributes so largely to its richness and effectiveness, and to those who say that a poet *should* concern himself merely with the sound or symbolic value of words we can only answer that, looking at the question in an elementary arithmetical way, it seems clear that he should *not* so pauperize himself.

. . . We have only to turn to a comprehensive anthology of English (or for that matter European) poetry to realize that all the recognized poetry which has been produced and preserved throughout our literary history uses as its medium not the secondary aspects of language alone, but these in conjunction with the intellectual meaning of words.

DAVID DAICHES: *The Place of Meaning in Poetry*, 1935

Art is always the product of *both* emotion and thought—not entirely emotion, for a purely emotional state is unstable and will interfere with any kind of creative effort.

RAY BETHERS: *Pictures, Painters and You*, 1953

The poet is neither an intellectual nor an emotional being alone; he feels his thoughts and thinks his sensations.

ELIZABETH DREW: *Discovering Poetry*, 1933

I feel strongly and I think strongly, but I seldom feel without thinking or think without feeling.

S. T. COLERIDGE: Letter, 17 December 1796

. . The flame of the passions, communicated to the imagination, reveals to us, with a flash of lightning, the inmost recesses of thought. . .

WILLIAM HAZLITT: *Lectures on the English Poets*, 1818

They [the mystical writers] contributed to keep alive the heart in the head.

S. T. COLERIDGE: *Biographia Literaria,* 1817

[The Elizabethan age] A period when the intellect was immediately at the tips of the senses. Sensation became word and word was sensation.

T. S. ELIOT: 'Philip Massinger' in *The Sacred Wood*, 1920

To feel Donne's poetry you have to think it.

HUGH I'ANSON FAUSSET

The quality in question is not peculiar to Donne and Chapman. In common with the greatest—Marlowe, Webster, Tourneur and Shakespeare—they had a quality of sensuous thought, or of thinking through the senses, or of the senses thinking. . . .

T. S. ELIOT, in essay on 'Imperfect Critics' in
The Sacred Wood, 1920

The basis and root of poetry is spontaneous utterance of the undivided being. It is not the utterance of thought, neither is it the utterance of emotion: it is the utterance of the being before these faculties are differentiated. . . . The conflict of Thought and Emotion is the beginning of self-consciousness; the conflict and the condition are really synonymous. Poetry is, essentially, prior to this conflict and condition; it is the utterance of a whole experience, which demands to be completed by utterance as whole as itself.

'O for a life of Sensations rather than of Thoughts', cried Keats; but because his saying is interpreted by the self-consciousness of beings whose Thoughts are divided against their Emotions, it is twisted into a cry for a life of Emotions rather than Thoughts. That is to misunderstand him completely. He is asking for a life of complete and undivided experiences.

J. MIDDLETON MURRY: *Shakespeare*, 1936

. . . the Imagination is not a separate faculty, nor does it supersede Thought and Emotion. It is the condition which obtains when Thought and Emotion have been brought into harmonious subordination to the Life from which their separate being is derived. A man imagines with his whole being. . . . We should conceive Imagination as Nature reasserting control over all the precious but overweening faculties which, though they derive from her, seek separately to establish a tyranny over her.

J. MIDDLETON MURRY: *The same*

❧ LOOSE EMOTION ❧

Bad writing is bad feeling.
S. T. COLERIDGE

Readers are often suspicious of emotion because some writers have over-indulged it. We dislike (as Professor Firkin puts it) the poem that puts up its mouth to be kissed. Feeling without thought is no more a prescription for true poetry than thought without feeling. It may give pleasure to the poet himself and to certain of his readers, but it is an inferior type of pleasure.

⊛　　⊛　　⊛

Sentimentality is at its worst in verse, when emotion flows over a theme, vague, and hazy and amorphous, with the non-inebriating quality of warm tea.

JOHN LIVINGSTON LOWES

The enemies of good verse . . . are sentimentality and rhetoric: feeling that suffers from elephantiasis and the expression of false feeling. Time forgives those by whom language lives because they will not deceive either their neighbours or themselves. . . . They bring language into accord with the truth of things.

BABETTE DEUTSCH: *New York Times Book Review*

The sentimentalist escapes the stern travail of thought. The poem is born in a sort of poetic twilight sleep.

JOHN LIVINGSTON LOWES

Poetry is not a turning loose of emotion, but an escape from emotion; it is not the expression of personality, but an escape from personality.

But, of course, only those who have personality and emotions know what it means to want to escape from these things.[1]

T. S. ELIOT: 'Tradition and Individual Talent',
The Sacred Wood, 1920

. . . Literature is so far not self-expression that it may more conveniently be conceived as a kind of self-*com*pression—a compression of the stuff of my individuality into forms of art.

H. W. GARROD: *Poetry and the Criticism of Life*, 1934

. . . it is not the 'greatness', the intensity of the emotions, the components, but the intensity of the artistic process, the pressure, so to speak, under which the fusion takes place, that counts.

T. S. ELIOT: 'Tradition and Individual Talent'

In true art the emotions are not only stirred; they are also brought into artistic relation with the other elements of the experience by the power of the poet's words. The emotions are held to the experience and worked into its unity. . . .

P. GURREY: *The Appreciation of Poetry*, 1935

---

[1] But isn't it as wrong to escape from emotion as to escape from thought? The antonym of 'turning loose' is to 'tame' or 'control'. We do not run away from the unbroken colt: we rope it in. And in poetry we rope in our emotions and make them work for our poem—without, in the process, we hope, breaking their spirit.

❧ CONTROLLED EMOTION ❧

. . . the struggle—which alone constitutes life for a poet—to
transmute his personal and private agonies into something
rich and strange, something universal and impersonal.
T. S. ELIOT, 'Shakespeare and the Stoicism of Seneca'

How, then, is the feeling to be controlled and worked into the unity
of the poem? Each poet must find his own salvation, but in some way
he has to remove himself from the emotion, stand outside and see it in
perspective. Time is one corrective:

❋　　❋　　❋

Only when they [our impressions and memories] have turned to blood
within us . . . can it happen that in a most rare hour the first word of a
poem arises in their midst and goes forth from them.

R. M. RILKE: *The Notebook of Malte Laurids Brigge*

I have a faculty . . . for burying an emotion in my heart or brain for
forty years, and exhuming it at the end of that time as fresh as when
interred.

THOMAS HARDY: Notebooks

Emotion recollected in tranquillity.

WILLIAM WORDSWORTH

It will not do to talk of 'emotion recollected in tranquillity': which is
only one poet's account of his recollection of his own methods.

T. S. ELIOT: Preface to *The Sacred Wood*, 1920

'Emotion recollected in tranquillity' is an inexact formula. For it is
neither emotion, nor recollection, nor, without distortion of meaning,
tranquillity. It is a concentration, and a new thing resulting from the

concentration of a very great number of experiences which to the practical and active person would not seem to be experiences at all; it is a concentration which does not happen consciously or of deliberation. These experiences are not 'recollected', and they finally unite in an atmosphere which is 'tranquil' only in that it is a passive attending upon the event.

T. S. ELIOT: 'Tradition and Individual Talent'

◉　　◉　　◉

In any case, not all poets have had time to allow Time to work on their emotions. They create a perspective by an immediate act of will: the stronger the emotion, the stronger the will needed to detach them. Wilfred Owen is such a poet.

◉　　◉　　◉

His poems are calm. In spite of the intense passion which is their impulse, they have a haunting serenity. For the poet has, at whatever cost, mastered his experience; his emotion has become tranquil. . . . It is not a comfortable peace, this joyless yet serene resignation; but it is a victory of the human spirit. We receive from it that exalted pleasure, that sense of being lifted above the sphere of anger and despair, which poetic imagination alone can give.

J. MIDDLETON MURRY: 'The Poet of the War', 1920,
The Evolution of an Intellectual

◉　　◉　　◉

Some poets—among them Browning and Eliot—find the solution by speaking through the mask of another character, or translating their experiences into other events and actions.

◉　　◉　　◉

The only way of expressing emotion in the form of art is by finding an 'objective correlative'; in other words, a set of objects, a situation, a chain of events, which shall be the formula of that *particular* emotion; such that when the external facts, which must terminate in sensory experience, are given, the emotion is immediately evoked.[1]

T. S. ELIOT: 'Hamlet and his Problems', 1920

[1] This is only one poet's account of his recollection of his own methods.

The end of art, whose essence is restraint, is not to make us grieve, or love, or hate, or flush with anger, or grow pale with rage. It is to stir us with the sense of an imperishable beauty. And that sense is communicated only when the poet has been first submerged and then detached, when he has passed out of the very torrent, tempest and whirlwind of passion. . . .

JOHN LIVINGSTON LOWES: *Convention and Revolt in Poetry*, 1919

✺ POETIC EMOTION ✺

*Impressions and experiences which are important for the
man may take no place in the poetry, and those which become
important in the poetry may play quite a negligible part in the
man, the personality.*
T. S. ELIOT, 'Tradition and Individual Talent'

Whatever the individual solution, the final result is the same in every
successful poem. The emotion is no longer the poet's personal emotion
alone: it has been universalised by the form of art. Nor is it any longer
that *type* of emotion alone: in the furnace of concentration, pain or
despair has been bent like a steel bar until it touches the other end of
happiness.

❀   ❀   ❀

. . . the feeling, or emotion, or vision, resulting from the poem is
something different from the feeling or emotion or vision in the
mind of the poet.

T. S. ELIOT: Preface to *The Sacred Wood*, 1920

Because he is an artist, his grief has become to him as living clay for
the potter's wheel. It must take form. And it can take form only when
it is looked back upon, or down upon, or through. And what we feel
is not grief at all, but a lofty tranquillity, a deep beauty, wrung from
grief, but no longer grief itself.

JOHN LIVINGSTON LOWES: *Convention and Revolt in Poetry*, 1919

. . . But the emotion, of whatever kind and in whatever degree, from
various causes, is qualified by various pleasures, so that in describing
any passions whatsoever, which are voluntarily described, the mind
will, upon the whole, be in a state of enjoyment.

WILLIAM WORDSWORTH: Preface to *Lyrical Ballads*,
Third Edition, 1802

[Lyrical poetry] succeeds in turning one poignant emotion into another poignant emotion, without introducing any modifying or transmuting elements. . . . The poetry is of course complex, however simple, for the reason suggested above; to take an emotion and express it in a vehement pattern of associative words, you have a different, though perhaps allied emotion. 'I would I were where Helen lies' is not the same thing as grief for Helen; it even in a sense contradicts it, for who would want to be where Helen lies while we can enjoy her death so marvellously?

CHARLES WILLIAMS: *Reason and Beauty in the Poetic Mind*, 1933

The original impressions of sense, whatever their character, the poet feels—because he is a poet—in a fashion more lively, more poignant, than ordinary men. But—and again because he is a poet—he more quickly establishes his tranquillity. Presently . . . it is

> Sorrow that is not sorrow, but delight,
> And miserable love that is not pain
> To hear of.

It is this purified passion that the poet conveys to those to whom he speaks; and hence that power which there is in poetry to console and sustain. The poet 'thinks and feels in the spirit of human passions'. *In the spirit of them*; for once more, let there be no mistake. It is in vain that we think and feel passionately—in vain for the purposes of poetic creation—unless this passion of thought and feeling has that in it by which it spiritualizes itself. Perhaps that is only another way of saying that the work of imagination can be done by the imagination only.

H. W. GARROD: *Wordsworth: Lectures and Essays*, 1927

I would distinguish . . . between human emotion and poetic passion. [He quotes some lines from Hardy.] The mood is of disillusionment; the ideas are turned wryly inside out, to demonstrate that there is no truth in them. But the reader receives no more of that disillusionment than is necessary to set off and embody the poetic emotion: he is not disillusioned, he is exhilarated.

C. DAY LEWIS: *The Poetic Image*, 1947

[After quoting stanzas from 'In Memoriam'.] But his regret for those things is not the strongest feeling the reader gets from the poem. It is the beauty and the glory of them that the reader chiefly feels. Sorrow has been turned into delight, even if the delight has a tinge of melancholy in it.

C. DAY LEWIS: *Poetry for You*, 1944

◎   ◎   ◎

In other words, by detaching himself from them, the poet is free of his emotions; and in some strange way, the poem is free of him. It has a life of its own, and starts out on its independent journey through men's minds.

◎   ◎   ◎

The poem's existence is somewhere between the writer and the reader: it has a reality which is not simply the reality of what the writer is trying to 'express', or of his experience of writing it, or of the experience of the reader, or of the writer as reader.

T. S. ELIOT: Introduction to *The Use of Poetry*, 1933

When personal poetry fails, it is because the personal experience from which it derives so possesses the poet's mind that he cannot see through it to the poetic experience: he is unwilling to sacrifice the personal meaning to the poetic meaning.

C. DAY LEWIS: *The Poetic Image*, 1947

There are many people who appreciate the expression of sincere emotion in verse, and there is a smaller number of people who can appreciate technical excellence. But very few know when there is expression of *significant* emotion, emotion which has its life in the poem and not in the history of the poet. The emotion of art is impersonal. And the poet cannot reach this impersonality without surrendering himself wholly to the work to be done.

T. S. ELIOT: 'Tradition and Individual Talent', 1920

Complete submission is an essential phase in that process of mastering the emotion with which the poet's creation begins, for the poet himself has to be changed; he plunges into the depths of his emotion to rise mysteriously renewed. Only then will the words he utters bear upon them the strange compulsion of a secret revealed; only then can he put his spell upon us and trouble our depths. For the problem of poetry is not primarily, or even largely, a conscious problem; true poetry begins with an act, a compelled and undeliberate act, of obedience to that centre of our being where all experience is reconciled.

J. MIDDLETON MURRY: 'The Poet of the War', 1920,
The Evolution of an Intellectual

✻ MEANING ✻

The proof of the purest poetry is that its
meaning is inexhaustible.
HUGH I'ANSON FAUSSET, *Poets and Pundits*

To consider the place of meaning in poetry is to be reminded before long very forcibly that thought and emotion are ultimately inseparable, that ideas are as effective as sights or sounds in producing emotional states of mind, and that the most intense state of human consciousness is when intellect and feeling are simultaneously stimulated by the same significant truth. It is a sign of decadence in art to depend only on one of these two methods of apprehension.

> DAVID DAICHES: *The Place of Meaning in Poetry*, 1935

The 'meaning' of a poem is not what it would mean if translated into prose, but what it means to each reader when he translates it into the terms of his own spiritual experience. Poetry is above all a way of using words to say things which could not possibly be said in any other way, things which in a sense do not *exist* till they are born (or re-born) in poetry. As Mr Middleton Murry has said, great poets are 'men who have uttered a truth so mysterious that it cannot be wrenched apart from the words in which they uttered it'.

> C. DAY LEWIS: *Enjoying Poetry*, 1947

In true poetry it is . . . impossible to express the meaning in any but its own words, or to change the words without changing the meaning.

> A. C. BRADLEY: *Oxford Lectures on Poetry*, 1909

Pure poetry is not the decoration of a preconceived and clearly defined matter: it springs from the creative impulse of a vague imaginative mass pressing for development and definition. If the poet already knew exactly what he meant to say, why should he write the poem? . . . For only its completion can reveal, even to him, exactly what he wanted.

D

When he began and while he was at work, he did not possess his meaning; it possessed him. . . . And this is the reason why such poems strike us as creations, not manufactures, and have the magical effect which mere decoration cannot produce. This is also the reason why, if we insist on asking for the meaning of such a poem, we can only be answered 'It means itself'.

A. C. BRADLEY: *Oxford Lectures on Poetry*, 1909

What Beethoven meant by his symphony, or Turner by his picture, was not something which you can name, but the picture and the symphony. Meaning they have, but *what* meaning can be said in no language but their own: and we know this, though some strange delusion makes us think the meaning has less worth because we cannot put it into words. Well, it is just the same with poetry. But because poetry *is* words, we vainly fancy that some other words than its own will express its meaning. And they will do so no more . . . than words will express the meaning of the Dresden Madonna.

A. C. BRADLEY: *the same*

One cardinal fact about great poetry . . . is that its main value lies in a process, not in a result. . . . We do not understand a great poem till we have felt it through and as far as possible recreated in ourselves the emotions which it originally carried.

GILBERT MURRAY: 'The Interpretation of
Ancient Greek Literature'

The meaning of a poem is not something else but itself, and that self is not the sum of the meaning of all the words, but the blend and fusion of them. In the alchemy of poetry the words form not a mechanical but a chemical mixture.

KATHARINE M. WILSON: *Sound and Meaning in
English Poetry*, 1930

To sum up the profoundest meaning of a great poem by a commonplace has an unpleasant air, bringing art into dangerous proximity to the Wayside Pulpit.

E. M. W. TILLYARD: *Poetry Direct and Oblique*,
revised edition, 1948

There is a type of student . . . who has a curious subconscious itch in
the presence of poetry; an itch for explaining it, in the hope of explaining it away.
                              G. K. CHESTERTON: *Chaucer*, 1932

The most dangerous enemies of poetry in general or of particular
groups of poets are those usually well-meaning people who go about
saying: 'What does it mean?' Such people are trying to divorce the
mental form, or rather a small part only of the mental form (the factual
content in its logical sequence) from the totality of the poem, the
unique whole that is made up of many mental and physical ingredients.
You cannot take an egg out of a cake that has been baked!
                   MARJORIE BOULTON: *The Anatomy of Poetry*, 1953

Poetry should speak directly to the emotions, and any attempt to hold
it up for interrogation on the threshold of self-consciousness will be
fatal. This is especially true for modern poetry, which is so commonly
approached by the reader with set teeth and a sombre determination
that at all costs he is not going to be baffled. Instead of reading it
aloud and letting the rhythm and images sink into his unconscious, he
worries it like a terrier, determined to extract a meaning out of it or die.
              C. DAY LEWIS: 'The Nurture of the Imagination',
                              Adult Education, December 1936

The chief use of the 'meaning' of a poem, in the ordinary sense, may
be . . . to satisfy one habit of the reader, to keep his mind diverted and
quiet, while the poem does its work upon him; much as the imaginary
burglar is always provided with a bit of nice meat for the house-dog.
              T. S. ELIOT: Conclusion to *The Use of Poetry*, 1933

People ordinarily incline to suppose that in order to enjoy a poem it is
necessary to 'discover its meaning'; so that their minds toil to discover
a meaning—a meaning which they can expound to anyone who will
listen, in order to prove that they enjoy it. But for one thing the possibilities of 'meaning' in poetry are so extensive that one is quite aware
that one's knowledge of the meaning even of what oneself has written
is extremely limited, and that its meaning to others . . . is quite as
much a part of it as what it means to oneself.
              T. S. ELIOT: Introduction to *The Wheel of Fire*
                              by G. Wilson Knight, 1930

What a poem means is as much what it means to others as what it means to the author; and indeed, in the course of time, a poet may become merely a reader in respect to his own works, forgetting his original meaning—or without forgetting, merely changing.

T. S. ELIOT: 'The Modern Mind',
The Use of Poetry, 1933

'Mr Eliot, when you wrote ".........." did you mean ".........."?'
'That was probably one of my meanings.'

T. S. ELIOT answering questions after one of his lectures

In all poetry there should be more than the author himself is aware of: the question of what the author meant or what a poem meant to the author when he was writing it, is itself a meaningless question. . . . In really creative writing the author is making something which he does not understand himself.

T. S. ELIOT: 'The Aims of Poetic Drama', *Adam*, 1951

Words do not have *either-or* meanings in imaginative poetry: they have *and-and-and* meanings. That is how poetry works.

HILARY CORKE: Letter to *The Listener*

The poem ['Cap and Bells'] has always meant a great deal to me, though . . . it has not always meant quite the same thing.

W. B. YEATS

I then observed Shakespeare standing between Betterton and Booth, and deciding a difference between those two great actors, concerning the placing of an accent in one of his lines: this was disputed on both sides with a warmth, which surprised me in Elysium, till I discovered by intuition that every soul retained its principal characteristics, being, indeed, its very essence. The line was that celebrated one in *Othello*:
'Put out the light, and then put out the light', according to Betterton. Mr Booth contended to have it thus:
'Put out the light, and then put out THE light'. I could not help offering my conjecture on this occasion, and suggested it might perhaps be:

'Put out the light, and then put out THEE, light'; making light to be the vocative case. Another would have altered the last word, and read,

'Put out thy light, and then put out thy sight.' But Betterton said, if the text was to be disturbed, he saw no reason why a word should not be changed as well as a letter, and instead of 'put out thy sight', you might read 'put out thy eyes'. At last it was agreed on all sides to refer the matter to the decision of Shakespeare himself, who delivered his sentiments as follows: 'Faith, gentlemen, it is so long since I wrote the line, I have forgot my meaning. This I know, could I have dreamt so much nonsense would have been talked and writ about it, I would have blotted it out of my works: for I am sure if any of these be my meaning, it doth me very little honour.'

HENRY FIELDING: *A Journey from this World to the Next*, 1783

✤ IMPLICATION ✤

*Poetry had far better imply things than preach them directly
. . . in the open pulpit her voice grows hoarse and fails.*
F. L. LUCAS, *Decline and Fall of the Romantic Ideal*

The business of words in prose is primarily to *state*; in poetry, not only to state, but also (and sometimes primarily) to *suggest*.

JOHN LIVINGSTON LOWES

Telling never dilates the mind with suggestion as implication does.

SEAN O'FAOLAIN: *The Short Story*, 1948

Pope and his contemporaries wrote brilliantly accomplished verse—verse that is often very pretty and very witty and always has that admirable lucidity which springs from a mastery of technique: on the other hand, it never suggests more than it actually says, and—as I conceive it to be—poetry is essentially that something more which cannot be said, but only suggested, communicated in some secret way as by the whispering of spirit to spirit.

FORREST REID: *The Milk of Paradise*, 1946

Poetry translates into its special sensory language a great deal that is given in the ordinary daily intercourse between minds by gesture, tones of voice, and expression. . . .

I. A. RICHARDS: *Practical Criticism*, 1929

Mallarmé in his *Divagations relativement au vers* pronounced uncompromisingly against all statement in poetry and for pure obliquity. . . . A good deal of recent English verse has accepted Mallarmé's doctrine to be oblique at any cost; with the result that some of it, naturally belonging to the province of statement, masquerades as obliquity. . . .

E. M. W. TILLYARD: *Poetry Direct and Oblique,*
revised edition, 1948

       ⊛   ⊛   ⊛

To summarize: although a poem needs a ballast of prose-meaning to prevent it from rising too far into the clouds, one that has too much ballast will never become airborne. The greatest poetry contains not so much 'meaning' as an *essence* of meaning—just as the knowledge it contains is a distillation of knowledge.

❧ KNOWLEDGE ❧

Poetry begins in delight and ends in wisdom.
ROBERT FROST

To be a poet is to have a soul . . . in which knowledge passes instantaneously into feeling, and feeling flashes back as a new organ of knowledge.

GEORGE ELIOT: *Middlemarsh,* 1872

The arresting and compelling power of genius must arise from knowledge; not so much from knowledge of facts which are learned from books, as from the knowledge that is acquired from sympathetic observation; and which leads, after a period of years, to a power which pierces to the heart of a subject with the swiftness and sureness of divination.

ROSAMOND HARDING: *An Anatomy of Inspiration,* 1948

This insight, which expresses itself by what is called Imagination, is a very high sort of seeing, which does not come by study, but by the intellect being where and what it sees; by sharing the path or circuit of things through forms, and so making them translucid to others.

R. W. EMERSON: Essay on 'The Poet'

[Plotinus] in the fifth book of the fifth Ennead, speaking of the highest and intuitive knowledge as distinguished from the discursive . . . says: 'It is not lawful to inquire from whence it sprang, as if it were a thing subject to place and motion, for it neither approached hither, nor again departs from hence to some other place, but it either appears to us or it does not appear. So that we ought not to pursue it with a view to detecting its secret source, but to watch in quiet till it suddenly shines upon us; preparing ourselves for the blessed spectacle as the eye waits patiently for the rising sun.'

S. T. COLERIDGE: *Biographia Literaria,* 1817

The true literary mind is likely to develop slowly; it needs a more comprehensive and more varied diet, a more miscellaneous knowledge of facts, a greater experience of men and of ideas, than the kind required for the practice of the other arts. It therefore presents a more baffling educational problem.

T. S. ELIOT: 'The Classics and the Man of Letters', 1942

It is important that the artist should be highly educated in his own art; but his education is one that is hindered rather than helped by the ordinary processes of society which constitute education for the ordinary man. For these processes consist largely in the acquisition of impersonal ideas which obscure what we really are and feel, what we really want, and what really excites our interest. It is of course not the actual information acquired, but the conformity which the accumulation of knowledge is apt to impose, that is harmful.

T. S. ELIOT: 'Blake', in *The Sacred Wood*, 1920

Those who accuse him [Shakespeare] to have wanted learning, give him the greater commendation: he was naturally learned; he needed not the spectacles of books to read nature; he looked inwards, and found her there.

JOHN DRYDEN: *An Essay on Dramatick Poesy*, 1668

While we persist in believing that a poet ought to know as much as will not encroach upon his necessary receptivity and necessary laziness, it is not desirable to confine knowledge to whatever can be put into a useful shape for examinations, drawing-rooms, or the still more pretentious modes of publicity. Some can absorb knowledge, the more tardy must sweat for it. Shakespeare acquired more essential history from Plutarch than most men could from the whole British Museum.

T. S. ELIOT: 'Tradition and Individual Talent'

Shakespeare wrote better poetry for not knowing too much. Milton, I think, knew too much finally for the good of his poetry.

ALFRED WHITEHEAD

 REASON

Reason has moons, but moons not hers
Lie mirrored in her sea,
Confounding her astronomers
But oh! delighting me.
                    RALPH HODGSON

I learned from him [James Bowyer] that poetry, even that of the loftiest and, seemingly, that of the wildest odes, had a logic of its own, as severe as that of science; and more difficult, because more subtle, more complex, and dependent on more, and more fugitive, causes.

                    S. T. COLERIDGE: *Biographia Literaria*, 1817

They [the French] will not consider that the imagination has its own laws, to which the understanding cannot and should not penetrate.

        J. W. GOETHE: *Conversations with Eckermann*, 5 July 1827

Of course a poem needs ultimately to cohere into some kind of sense; but the sense it makes will be imaginative sense rather than intellectual sense—appealing to a different part of our understanding from our reason. It is a matter of what I should call heart-logic, as distinct from head-logic.

    MARGARET WILLY:'The Nature of Poetry',
                    an address to the English Association, 1956

Reason is the enumeration of qualities already known; imagination is the perception of the value of those qualities, both separately and as a whole. . . . Reason is to the imagination as the instrument to the agent, as the body to the spirit, as the shadow to the substance. . . .

            P. B. SHELLEY: *A Defence of Poetry*, 1820

... shaping fantasies that apprehend
More than cool reason ever comprehends.

WILLIAM SHAKESPEARE: *Midsummer Night's Dream*,
Act V, Sc. 1

Is it by an act of will or by the exercise of reason that we take pleasure in colour and form and pattern, an acorn, a rainbow, a tree in the wind, a dancer at rest; that we delight in beauty, welcome goodness, recognize truth, acquire ideals, choose our friends, or fall, and stay, in love? Or even, for that matter, see a joke?

WALTER DE LA MARE: 'Dream and Imagination',
Behold This Dreamer, 1939

In the vision of God, what one sees is not the reason, but something prior to and superior to the reason.

PLOTINUS

❀　　❀　　❀

In our reaction against the attempted domination of reason, however, we need to guard against its rejection. Otherwise we may come to accept as poetry any piece of automatic writing or complacent surrealism which happens to satisfy the author.

❀　　❀　　❀

It is nonsense to think that a flight from reason is necessarily an advance towards a more powerful imaginative life. The discipline of the intellectual life is an altogether saving factor in any culture worthy of its name.

D. J. JAMES: *Scepticism and Poetry*, 1937

Today for a variety of reasons many people are not only reluctant to think for themselves, but ready to congratulate themselves on their disinclination to do so. They will pronounce, not with sorrow, but with relief or rage, such views as 'Reason has failed' or 'Science can tell us nothing of fundamental importance'; and by these statements they will mean more than 'Reason and science are not able to tell us everything that we should like to know'. There are often distinct undertones declaring that reason is wicked or out of date, and a kind of joy is felt in making the assertion that science is 'only' a list of measurements. Such obscurantism is not only stupid but dangerous, and is the more dangerous for being fashionable. Reason, throughout history, has often played the part of a devil revolting against God, and the liberating part has often been overplayed; but whenever reason has been driven out, seven worse devils have immediately filled the empty room.

REX WARNER in *The London Magazine*, February 1954

It was well said by Aristotle, 'that the mind hath over the body that commandment which the lord hath over the bondman; but that reason hath over the imagination that commandment which a magistrate hath over a free citizen', who may come also to rule in his turn. For we see that in matters of Faith and Religion, we raise our Imagination above our Reason; which is the cause why Religion sought ever access to the mind by similitudes, types, parables, visions, dreams.

FRANCIS BACON: quoted in *Behold This Dreamer*

⊛   ⊛   ⊛

Verse that makes no use of reason is likely to be chaotic and must eventually cease to communicate. On the other hand, work that makes sole use of reason and neglects emotion and imagination may be formally correct yet spiritually dead—like so much verse of the eighteenth century. Reason must be present in poetry, but it must be Wordsworth's 'divine reason'—reason that is warm, not cold, reason that is prepared to follow where imagination leads. If not, the mind will stop short at the borders of the already-mapped, and never take that leap into the unknown which constitutes poetic faith.

⊛   ⊛   ⊛

Imagination is not necessarily opposed to reason, but it begins where reason leaves off.

CLIVE SANSOM: *Poetry and Religious Experience*, 1948

To be a poet is to have a heightened awareness of unity. And this, again, is to become concerned with conceptions which cannot be effectively expressed in terms of analytical thought. It is, indeed, just the office of the poet to bring to life for us those aspects of existence with which the imagination alone can deal. It follows inescapably, therefore, that any philosophy which has its roots in the poetic consciousness must exhibit an anti-rationalistic tendency. That is to say, it will utilize all the resources of reason to substantiate the fact that this nature of Reality cannot be fully apprehended by the exercise of the reason alone.

LAWRENCE HYDE: *The Prospects of Humanism*, 1931

Poets try to express experience, not as the mind orders and arranges it in retrospect, but as it is really felt with all its contradictions and ambiguities, and this too has led to misrepresentation. This poetry has been accused of being deliberately anti-rational because it speaks of irrational things without attempting to simplify them. But the business of poetry is not to simplify or to explain, but to present. Things should be presented as they are, and to complain that if a poet does this he is an enemy of reason is to say that truth itself is anti-rational. The fact is that poetry is neither rational nor irrational, since it is concerned not with the reasoning powers of man but with something else, with the whole range of the human consciousness when it is at work at a certain intensity.

C. M. BOWRA: *The Creative Experiment*, 1949

✣ PHILOSOPHY ✣

Philosophy will clip an Angel's wings,
Conquer all mysteries by rule and line,
Empty the haunted air . . .
JOHN KEATS, 'Lamia'

Philosophy, or constructive thought about the nature of life, is a danger when the creative writer regards it as an end in itself instead of a stimulus to his imagination.

Review of *Alfred de Vigny* by Emile Lauvrière,
in the *Times Literary Supplement*

. . . axioms in philosophy are not axioms until they are proved upon our pulses.

JOHN KEATS in a letter to John Hamilton Reynolds, 3 May 1818

The great writer does not really come to conclusions about life; he discerns a quality in it.

J. MIDDLETON MURRY: *The Problem of Style*, 1922

Poetry to Philosophy: 'But if you address yourself to Man, you will find that his business is not at all to *comprehend* the Universe, for this, if he could achieve it, would make him equal with God. What he more humbly aspires to, is to *apprehend*. . . .'

A. QUILLER COUCH: Essay on 'Poetry'

Poetry . . . is not the *expression* of ideas or of a view of life; it is their discovery or creation.

A. C. BRADLEY

A poem does not admit argumentation, though it does admit development of thought.

S. T. COLERIDGE: *Table Talk*, 21 July 1832

Without doubt, the effort of the philosopher proper, the man who is trying to deal with ideas in themselves, and the effort of the poet, who may be trying to *realize* ideas, cannot be carried on at the same time. But this is not to deny that poetry can be in some sense philosophic. The poet can deal with philosophic ideas, not as matter for argument, but as matter for inspection.

T. S. ELIOT: on Dante, in *The Sacred Wood*, 1920

What his [Blake's] genius required, and what it sadly lacked, was a framework of accepted and traditional ideas which would have prevented him from indulging in a philosophy of his own, and concentrated his attention upon the problems of the poet.

T. S. ELIOT: Essay on William Blake, 1920

Didactic poetry is my abhorrence; nothing can be equally well expressed in prose that is not tedious and so superogatory in verse.

P. B. SHELLEY: Preface to *Prometheus Unbound*, 1820

Didacticism is to be criticized in poetry, not because the content does not matter, but because the only thing that does matter is that part of the content which the poet's imagination has transformed. In other words, when the imagination has fused its material, the question how far this is also didactic does not arise.

OSBERT BURDETT: *The Brownings*, 1928

. . . To value poetry for its message or the nature of its philosophical content is to misunderstand its very nature. If we truly care for poetry and know the virtue to be found in it, we shall profit equally from Wordsworth, who tells us that 'Our birth is but a sleep and a forgetting', and from Swinburne, who tells us 'This life is a watch or a vision between a sleep and a sleep', and Browning, who holds that 'We fall to rise, are baffled to fight better, sleep to wake'. Here we have three poets coming to three vastly different conclusions upon much the same speculation, but that does not matter. The point is that each in turn has been able to see his own philosophical experience so clearly that he has been able to reduce it to this excellent clarity of form, and it is that shaping faculty which stimulates our faculty to its own rich purpose in turn.

JOHN DRINKWATER: *The Poet and Communication*, 1923
Conway Memorial Lecture of the South Place Ethical Society

The test of its poetic value for us lies simply in the question whether it satisfies our imagination; the rest of us, our knowledge or conscience, for example, judging it only so far as they appear transmuted in our imagination. So also Shakespeare's knowledge or his moral insight, Milton's greatness of soul, Shelley's 'hate of hate' and 'love of love', and that desire to help men or make them happier which may have influenced a poet in hours of meditation—all these have, as such, no poetical worth: they have that worth only when, passing through the unity of the poet's being, they reappear as qualities of imagination.

A. C. BRADLEY: *Oxford Lectures on Poetry*, 1909

The quality of the imagination is to flow, and not to freeze. The poet did not stop at the colour or the form, but read their meaning; neither may he rest in this meaning, but he makes the same objects exponents of his new thought. Here is the difference betwixt the poet and the mystic, that the last nails a symbol to one sense, which was a true sense for a moment, but soon becomes old and false. For all symbols are fluxional; all language is vehicular and transitive, and is good, as ferries and horses are, for conveyance, not as farms and houses are, for homestead.

R. W. EMERSON: Essay on 'The Poet'

Most people now agree that poetry has a moral effect, but in order to mould our character and attitudes in its own indirect fashion it must at least be poetry, and this it seldom is when it becomes openly and merely didactic. It is just here that so much literary criticism, and especially so many Ph.D. theses go wrong. They go wrong by treating a poet's 'thought' as if it were something which could be detached from the poetry, and discussed as part of the history of philosophy or ethics. To such critics and researchers, indeed, the poetry is a positive nuisance; it is just so much shell to be cracked and rejected in order to get at the nut of prose-meaning inside. If this nut were the only thing that mattered, the poet would have saved endless trouble by handing it to us in plain prose, like a man and a philosopher, instead of padding it round with a lot of obscure rhetoric.

BASIL WILLEY: Broadcast Talk, 'Poetry and Philosophy'
The Listener, 2 February 1950

The slightest personal experience of the spirit is worth, *as poetry*, more than all the greatest ideas of the world's greatest teachers repeated with no matter how much reverence.

'A. E.' [GEORGE RUSSELL]: *The Living Torch*, 1937

MORALS, POLITICS
AND ETHICS

We hate poetry that has a palpable design upon us—and if we do
not agree, seems to put a hand in its breeches pocket.
JOHN KEATS, in a letter to John Hamilton Reynolds

Poetry is not concerned with telling people what to do, but with ex-
tending our knowledge of good and evil, perhaps making the necessity
for action more urgent and its nature more clear, but only leading us
to the point where it is possible to make a rational and moral choice.

W. H. AUDEN: Introduction to *The Poet's Tongue*, 1935

Poetry does not move us to be just or unjust, in itself. It moves us to
thoughts in whose light justice and injustice are seen in fearful sharpness
of outline. J. BRONOWSKI: *The Poet's Defence*, 1939

It is not the poet's business to save man's soul, but to make it worth
saving. JAMES ELROY FLECKER

The poet is a sensitive instrument, not a leader.

C. DAY LEWIS: *A Hope for Poetry*, 1936

The mission of poetry is to record impressions, not convictions.

THOMAS HARDY: Notebooks

Poetry does not teach us, but it allows us to be taught, as life and the
universe permit us, if we will, to learn. The poet's sense of ethical
values, if he has it, may communicate itself to us, as Shakespeare's does,
implicitly, without the intrusion of a moral sentiment.

JOHN LIVINGSTON LOWES:
Convention and Revolt in Poetry, 1919

E

Many 'poetry lovers' would be shocked if we told them that they do not really love poetry at all: what they love is the prose meaning they can extract from a poem, or its 'message': many of the Victorians, for instance, and the devotees of our political poetry of the thirties, were asking poets to give them a substitute for their own lost faith, or a guide to action, or a new set of values, or a sense of human purpose in an apparently mechanistic universe. Poetry may of course produce any of these effects, and remain poetry; but they are still by-products.

C. DAY LEWIS: *Enjoying Poetry*, 1947

If a poet would influence politics he must join a party, and then he is lost as a poet: goodbye to his free spirit and his open mind. . . . The poet as a man and a citizen will love his native land, but the native land of his genius lies in the world of goodness, greatness and beauty, a country without frontiers or boundaries, ready for him to seize and shape wherever he finds it.

J. W. GOETHE: *Conversations with Eckermann*, 1832

I do not mean to disparage the artist when I state the fact of his loose relation to morality, and accordingly to politics and the social problem. Never should I blame an artist who declared that reforming the world's morals were no business of his. The artist, he would say, 'improves' the world not by moral precepts but by quite different means: improves it by endowing it with spirit and meaning. He uses thought, word and image to set down his own life, and, figuratively, life as a whole. His task is to animate—just that and nothing more.

Goethe—who says the right thing in the most charming manner about most things in the world—says straight out: 'A work of art may have a moral effect, but to demand moral purpose from the artist is to make him ruin his job.'

THOMAS MANN: Broadcast Talk, 'The Artist and
Society', *The Listener*, 5 June 1952

Mrs Barbauld once told me that she admired the Ancient Mariner very much, but that there were two faults in it—it was improbable and had no moral. As for the probability, I owned that that might admit some question; but as to the want of a moral, I told her that in my own judgement the poem had too much; and that the only, or chief fault, if I might say so, was the obtrusion of the moral sentiment so openly on the reader as a principle or cause of action in a work of such pure imagination. It ought to have had no more moral than the Arabian Nights' tale of the merchant's sitting down to eat dates by the side of a well, and throwing the shells aside, and lo! a genie starts up and says he *must* kill the aforesaid merchant *because* one of the date shells had, it seems, put out the eye of the genie's son.

s. t. COLERIDGE: *Table Talk*, 31 May 1830

Coleridge is not . . . concerned with the prevention of cruelty to albatrosses. OLIVER ELTON: *A Survey of English Literature*

> For God's sake steer clear of verse
> Which wants to heal the universe.
>
> *Author unknown*

⊛ ⊛ ⊛

G. K. Chesterton, in one of his books, suggests that Shaw could not see the greatness of Shakespeare because he was looking for "that ghastly thing" which people call a Message—"and continue to call a Message even when they have become atheists and do not know who the Message is from".

⊛ ⊛ ⊛

The instructions conveyed in it [The Cumberland Beggar] are too direct and like a lecture: they don't slide into the mind of the reader, while he is imagining no such matter. . . . This fault, if I am right, is in a ten-thousandth worse degree to be found in Sterne and many novelists and modern poets who continually put a signpost up to show where you are to feel.

CHARLES LAMB: Letter to Wordsworth, January 1801

A moral should be wrought into the body and soul, the matter and tendency, of a poem, not tagged to the end, like a 'God send the good ship into harbour' at the conclusion of our bills of lading.

CHARLES LAMB: Letter to Southey

The poet who sets up a principle or ideal or policy which prevents him from accepting life as it is, limits himself and creates a false picture of life. STEPHEN SPENDER: *Life and the Poet*, 1942

The virtues common to good living and good poetry seem to me not so much matters of what used to be called 'virtue' as, above all, of sane vitality.

F. L. LUCAS: *Decline and Fall of the Romantic Ideal*, 1936

I affirm, Sir, that Poetry, that the imagination, generally speaking, delights in power, in strong excitement, as well as in truth, in good, in right, whereas pure reason and the moral sense approve only of the true and good.

JOHN KEATS in a letter to George and Georgiana Keats,
February–May 1819

If there be a moral in the subject, it will appear, and the poet has nothing to consider but the effective and artistic treatment of his subject. If a poet has as high a soul as Sophocles, his influence will always be moral, let him do what he will.

J. W. GOETHE: *Conversations with Eckermann*, March 1827

We must not place in antithesis poetry and human good, for poetry is one kind of human good; and . . . we must not determine the intrinsic value of this kind of good by direct reference to another.

A. C. BRADLEY: *Oxford Lectures on Poetry*, 1909

. . . the honors paid by Man to Man are trifles in comparison to the Benefit done by great Works to the Spirit and pulse of good by their mere passive existence.

JOHN KEATS in a letter to John Hamilton Reynolds,
19 February 1818

Creating a work of art is as direct a means to good as a human being can practise.

CLIVE BELL

⊛   ⊛   ⊛

Lastly, in case in our efforts to deny morality as a measuring-stick for poetry, we seem to be denying morality itself, a quotation which sets it in perspective.

⊛   ⊛   ⊛

Nobility, intensity, courage, generosity, pity—qualities like these cannot by themselves make a poem good, any more than they can make a
face beautiful. . . . But in a poem, as in a face, no perfection of form in
their absence can reach the highest beauty. And in a poem, as in a face,
the presence of their opposites—of vulgarity or morbidity or pol-
troonery or meanness or cruelty—is a flaw for which no perfection of
form can atone.

F. L. LUCAS: *The Decline and Fall of the Romantic Ideal,* 1936

❧ RELIGION AND BELIEF ❧

Religion is sometimes lugged in . . .
CHARLES LAMB, in a letter to Bernard Barton on his *Poetic Vigils*

Poetry is at bottom a criticism of life.

MATTHEW ARNOLD

Arnold might just as well have said that Christian worship is at bottom a criticism of the Trinity.

T. S. ELIOT

Nobody . . . talked more dogmatically about poetry than Matthew Arnold did, yet to my mind nobody ever explained it less. From beginning to end, the famous essay on 'The Study of Poetry' is really occupied much less with what poetry is than with what Arnold desired it to be: 'a criticism of life', an answer to the question, 'How to live?' Now poetry may or may not answer this question, but can we truthfully claim that it is less poetical if it doesn't?

FORREST REID: *The Milk of Paradise*, 1946

I see no valid reason for debarring dogma from poetry, if dogma is the best grist for your particular mill. One asks nothing of a mill except that what comes out at the other end should be, not grist, but flour. Doctrinal verse, didactic verse are very well; but they are not poetry, unless the moral truths have been translated into poetic truth. This, I realize, may be taken as an elaborate way of saying that poetry is not poetry unless it is poetry.

C. DAY LEWIS: *The Poet's Task*, 1951

It is not—in spite of Wordsworth's prose—the primal duty of poetry directly to encourage, exhort, or console. That it may do by the way, if we choose to take it so; but to make it the chief purpose is to turn poetry into a compensation for something lacked or lost, and, valuable as compensations are, poetry is too great for such a secondary business.

CHARLES WILLIAMS: *Reason and Beauty*
in the Poetic Mind, 1933

The attempt to make poetry serve a cause or interest is likely to deprive it of the freedom without which it cannot arrive at its particular kind of truth. For interests and causes see existence through blinkers; they distort being in order to achieve their ends. Poetry cannot take sides except with life.

STEPHEN SPENDER: *Life and the Poet*, 1942

Besides, men who read from religious or moral inclinations, even when the subject is of that kind which they approve, are beset with misconceptions and mistakes peculiar to themselves. Attaching so much importance to the truths which interest them, they are prone to overrate the authors by whom those truths are expressed and enforced. They come prepared to impart so much passion to the poet's language that they remain unconscious how little, in fact, they receive from it.

WILLIAM WORDSWORTH: Supplementary essay
to *Lyrical Ballads*, 1815

And certainly poetry is not the inculcation of morals, or the direction of politics; and no more is it religion or an equivalent of religion, except by some monstrous abuse of words.

T. S. ELIOT: Preface to *The Sacred Wood*, 1920

Poetry, as T. S. Eliot has said, is never a substitute for religion. Nor is religion a substitute for poetry. Each has its own purpose and value, its own justification. But if we could search for the experiences which produced them—the source of religion and the source of poetry—we might find ourselves exploring, if not the same ground, at least territories very close together.

That is why we need to distinguish between 'religion' and 'religious experience'. Religious experience is something that brings with it a sense of relationship with God—a connection of one's own life with a life outside oneself. It is at once a going-out of one's spirit, and an inpouring of some immeasurably greater spirit—a sense of commingling and union, of spiritual awareness. It is not primarily a matter of thought or morality. Religion, on the other hand, being an explanation

of that experience, is concerned very largely with thought and morality. It is an attempt to reconcile the spontaneous knowledge of the
spirit with the accumulated knowledge of the mind, of belief with
reasno. And, at the same time, it tries to reconcile what belongs to an
eternal level of existence with our normal everyday life in the world of
time.

Something similar is true of 'poetic experience' and 'poetry'. The
experience again is not mainly intellectual, but imaginative. Like
religious experience, too, it brings with it a heightened awareness and
a sense of unity. Poetry grows out of this poetic experience, as religion
out of religious experience, but instead of rationalizing its experience
and relating it to rules of conduct, poetry tries to communicate the
experience itself. It does not use words to persuade the reader or
listener towards belief (except belief in the validity of the experience).
It simply encourages him to share the poet's awareness. Because he has
shared it, the reader may be moved to action or to change of character,
but poetry written deliberately to inculcate morals or to influence conduct is seldom successful. It belongs to the sphere of ethics and philosophy rather than that of poetry.

CLIVE SANSOM: *Poetry and Religious Experience*, 1948

If we, as readers, keep our religious and moral convictions in one com-
partment, and take our reading merely for entertainment, or on a
higher plane for aesthetic pleasure, I would point out that the author,
whatever his conscious intentions in writing, in practice recognises no
such distinctions. The author of a work of imagination is trying to
affect us wholly, as human beings, whether he knows it or not; and we
are affected by it as human beings, whether we intend to be or not.

T. S. ELIOT: 'Religion and Literature',
Faith That Illuminates, 1935

＊　　＊　　＊

The operative word appears to be 'wholly'. If the *whole* poet is writing,
if his moral and religious beliefs are wholly assimilated in the creative
process of the poem, well and good. But if they have not been assimilated—if the poet writes as an atheist, a Quaker, or a churchwarden—
the result may provide excellent material for his fellow-worshippers,
but it is unlikely to be poetry of the highest order. And the more
widely known his religious attachments, the more difficult he may find
it to remain a free agent, a creative spirit with the whole field of
human thought before him.

＊　　＊　　＊

When a poet thinks, he must think as a poet. If he thinks as an adherent of any creed, he comes under Touchstone's anathema—he is damned, like an ill-roasted egg, all on one side. He is versifying his ideas, such as they are, not impregnating thought with imaginative beauty—which is one at least of poetry's high prerogatives.

JOHN LIVINGSTON LOWES: *Convention and Revolt in Poetry*, 1919

Poetry may have an ulterior value as a means to culture or religion; because it conveys instruction, or softens the passions, or furthers a good cause; because it brings the poet fame or money or a quiet conscience. So much the better: let it be valued for these reasons, too. But its ulterior worth neither is nor can directly determine its poetic worth as a satisfying imaginative experience, and this is to be judged entirely from within. . . . The consideration of ulterior ends, whether by the poet in the act of composing or by the reader in the act of experiencing, tends to lower poetic value. It does so because it tends to change the nature of poetry by taking it out of its own atmosphere. For its nature is to be not a part, nor yet a copy, of the real world (as we commonly understand that phrase), but to be a world by itself, independent, complete, autonomous; and to possess it fully you must enter that world, conform to it laws, and ignore for the time the beliefs, aims, and particular conditions which belong to you in the other world of reality.

A. C. BRADLEY: *Oxford Lectures on Poetry*, 1909

It has been argued that Browning, Keats, Wordsworth, Shelley—to mention only a few of our greater poets—were all mystics of one form or another. It is safer to say that mystical thought appealed to them as valuable poetic material.

A. R. ENTWISTLE: 'Mysticism in English Poetry',
The Study of Poetry, 1928

✺ THE SUSPENSION OF ✺ DISBELIEF

... that willing suspension of disbelief for the moment, which constitutes poetic faith.

S. T. COLERIDGE, *Biographia Literaria*

Coleridge, when he remarked that a 'willing suspension of disbelief' accompanied much poetry, was noting an important fact, but not quite in the happiest terms, for we are neither aware of a disbelief nor voluntarily suspending it in these cases. It is better to say that the question of belief or disbelief, in the intellectual sense, never arises when we are reading well.

I. A. RICHARDS: *Practical Criticism*, 1929

I am not a Buddhist, but some of the early Buddhist scriptures affect me as parts of the Old Testament do; I can still enjoy Fitzgerald's *Omar*, though I do not hold that rather smart and shallow view of life.

T. S. ELIOT: 'Shelley and Keats',
The Use of Poetry, 1933

The poetic world is a world without prejudices. The writ of those moral and practical judgments which we feel compelled to exercise elsewhere does not run here. We have even left behind those judgments as to reality and unreality without which we cannot elsewhere feel safe. But here an impression has only to be vivid enough in order to justify itself. This is the world in which Macbeth, on the brink of his crime, alarms us with the fear that his wickedness may not succeed. This is the world in which the villainy of Iago delights us with its refinement and resource. This is the world in which Ariel and Titania, Circe and Armida, Polyphemus and Fafnir, Satan and Prometheus, are figures which we accept as easily as the man next door; and the instant we ask ourselves whether such figures really exist or can exist, we are aware that in the very act of asking that question we have come clean out of the world of poetry.

LASCELLES ABERCROMBIE: *The Theory of Poetry*, 1924

If you deny the theory that full poetic appreciation is possible without belief in what the poet believed, you deny the existence of 'poetry' as well as 'criticism'; and if you push this denial to its conclusion, you will be forced to admit that your appreciation of it will be a function of your philosophy or theology or something else.

T. S. ELIOT: *Dante*, 1929

Several things dove-tailed in my mind, and at once it struck me what quality went to form a Man of Achievement, especially in Literature, and which Shakespeare possessed so enormously—I mean *Negative Capability*, that is, when a man is capable of being in uncertainties, mysteries, doubts, without any irritable reaching after fact and reason —Coleridge, for instance, would let go by a fine isolated verisimilitude caught from the Penetralium of mystery, from being incapable of remaining content with half-knowledge. This pursued through volumes would perhaps take us no further than this, that with a great poet the sense of Beauty overcomes every other consideration, or rather obliterates all consideration.

JOHN KEATS in a letter to George and
Thomas Keats, 21 December 1817

❧ SUBJECT MATTER ❧

. . . at bottom no real object is unpoetical if the poet knows how to use it properly.
J. W. GOETHE, *Conversations with Eckermann*

No subject remains trivial when the poetic imagination has done with it.

C. DAY LEWIS

A poem on a flea may be a very good poem, and a poem on the immortality of the soul may be a very bad poem.

ELIZABETH DREW: *Discovering Poetry*, 1933

Poetry—the art for which mountain and mouse, flea and elephant are of equal value.

C. DAY LEWIS

To poetry, as to Peter on the housetop, nothing is common or unclean.

JOHN LIVINGSTON LOWES: Notes to *The Road to Xanadu*, 1930

Extract poetry from anything you please: it lies in everything and everywhere.

GUSTAVE FLAUBERT

The great beauty of Poetry is, that it makes every thing every place interesting.

JOHN KEATS in a letter to George and
Georgiana Keats, September 1819

The essential virtue of poetry is resident, not in its matter, but in the power that moulds brute matter into form.

JOHN LIVINGSTON LOWES: *The Road to Xanadu*, 1930

How can the subject determine the value when on one and the same subject poems may be written of all degrees of merit and demerit; or when a perfect poem may be composed on a subject so slight as a pet sparrow and, if Macaulay may be trusted, a nearly worthless poem on a subject so stupendous as the omnipresence of the Deity?

A. C. BRADLEY: 'Poetry for Poetry's Sake',
Oxford Lectures on Poetry, 1909

No: we are not to dictate to an artist either subject or treatment, nor are we to deny to him any subject or any treatment. We are not schoolmistresses. We are not censors. All that matters is that the subject be one that awakens the artist's æsthetic passion, and that the harmony between subject and treatment be such that it casts a spell upon him, enabling him to be visited by his god, and so casts a spell upon us, enabling us to be visited by ours.

CHARLES MORGAN: 'The Artist and the Community',
Liberties of the Mind, 1951

One might define a creative writer of genius as one with the greatest power of seeing what is extraordinary within what is ordinary. The lesser artists are those who need the stimulus of what is surprising and in itself poetic, to create the poetic in art.

STEPHEN SPENDER: *Life and the Poet*, 1942

The old themes are perennial. Love is as dazzling a miracle to every lover who loves today as if unnumbered millions hadn't loved since time began. Death isn't trite to you and me because it's been the common lot since life first was; nor have the moon and stars grown old because uncounted centuries ago, beside the rivers of Babylon and Egypt, or among the hills and pasturelands of Israel, or in the wide stillness of Arabia, men saw them, and brooded, and wondered, and dreamed. The oldest things in the world are the things that also have been new as many times as human beings have been born.

JOHN LIVINGSTON LOWES: *Convention and Revolt in Poetry*, 1919

Most of the discussions that go on between rival schools of critics and poets are about unreal issues. One party announces that literature should be written about certain subjects in a certain way. All poetry about slums, dreams, gods, kings, nature, is said to be bad or good according to the fashion of the time. . . . Yet all the time it is a truism that it does not matter what the poetry is about or how it is written so long as it is well written and real. There are many doors that lead into life, and it does not matter whether you go by the front or the back entrance. The rare and genuine thing is to get there at all.

STEPHEN SPENDER: *Life and the Poet*, 1942

It is not good art to write badly about aeroplanes and automobiles, nor is it necessarily bad art to write well about the past.

Preface to *Some Imagist Poets*, 1915

We are just emerging from a period when it was considered that anything ordinary—for instance, an old boot—was not a fit subject for poetry. Modern poets have tended to go to the other extreme and to consider that old boots are the only subject for poetry.

E. W. F. TOMLIN: Lectures on Modern Poetry,
Speech Fellowship, 1936

If imagination, instead of being caught in wheels and pistons, penetrates to whatever of human glory of motion, daring of flight, beauty and terror and power is bound up with invention and the processes of modern life, then aeroplanes and railways, and wireless telegraphy, and all the rest, become fit matter for its exercise. . . . Until objects have become part and parcel of the loves, and hates, and hopes, and fears of men, they are not plastic stuff for art to work with.

JOHN LIVINGSTON LOWES: *Convention and*
Revolt in Poetry, 1919

Faith without works is not more dead than the loftiest themes of poetry may be, *as poetry*, if they have not been drenched in the creative deeps, and fashioned afresh by that architectonic energy which is the effluence of the creative will.

JOHN LIVINGSTON LOWES: *The Road to Xanadu*, 1930

＊   ＊   ＊

But the author goes on to state a most important truth, and one from which we may retreat too far in our reaction from the moralists—that *given* those depths and that energy, the higher theme is likely to produce the greater poetry:

'I am dying, Egypt, dying' stirs depths that the mariner's plummet never sounded, and touches heights beyond the zenith of the moving moon. But it does so because, in the tragic and glorious conception of which it is an integral portion, the same synthetic and magical power[1] which swept the multitudinous pageantry of the four elements within the frame of 'The Ancient Mariner' has there been exercised upon facts of nobler import and a larger mould.

JOHN LIVINGSTON LOWES: *The Road to Xanadu*, 1930

[1] Coleridge.

❧ BEAUTY ❧

*Beauty is the complexion of health. To reach it, we must put
aside our pre-occupation about different sorts of rouge.*
W. R. LETHABY, *Architecture*

To divide subjects into two groups, the beautiful or elevating, and the
ugly or vicious, and to judge poems according as their subjects belong
to one of these groups or the other, is to . . . confuse with our pre-
conceptions the meaning of the poet. What the thing is in the poem,
he is to be judged by, not by the thing as it was before he touched it;
and how can we venture to say beforehand that he cannot make a true
poem out of something which to us was merely alluring or dull or
revolting?

A. C. BRADLEY: 'Poetry for Poetry's Sake',
Oxford Lectures on Poetry, 1909

The poets of the nineteenth century were on the whole guided by a
belief in the Beautiful, and held that some subjects are beautiful in
themselves and others not, but the moderns are not very much interested in the Beautiful as such, and do not believe that there is a category
of beautiful subjects. What matters is the imaginative appeal of a subject, and there is no means by which this can be forecast in advance. So
mysterious indeed are the workings of the creative spirit that it may
find its subject in almost any field of experience. And this surely is true.
The devotees of Beauty rejected much that Shakespeare or Dante
would have accepted without question. What matters to the modern
poet is the essential excitement, the exaltation and thrill which he finds,
not a preconceived, general notion of what the subjects of poetry are
or are not.

C. M. BOWRA: *The Creative Experiment*, 1949

No artist strives less for beauty than the one who is in love with Nature.
Indifferent artists try to derive an advantage from the beauty of their
subject.

MAX FRIEDLANDER: *On Art and Connoisseurship*, 1942

A true poet does not trouble about the poetical—in the same way as a horticulturist does not scent his roses.

> JEAN COCTEAU: quoted by Edith Sitwell
> in *A Poet's Notebook*, 1943

Beauty is a bye-product.

> ALDOUS HUXLEY

Art is doing the right thing in the right way, and beauty is the evidence of it.

> W. R. LETHABY

I doubt whether an artist aims consciously at producing beauty. I try to express the character of what I am depicting. . . . The danger is the man who aims consciously at beauty, destroying all character.

> JACOB EPSTEIN: *The Sculptor Speaks*,
> quoted by Dr P. Gurrey

What we find beautiful in a work of art is not found beautiful by the eye, but by our imagination through the eye.

> GOTTHOLT LESSING: *Laöcoon: The Limits of
> Painting and Poetry*, 1766

A wrong note in 'God Save the King' seems ugly. It is only ugly in that particular context.

> E. W. F. TOMLIN

The contemplation of the horrid or sordid or disgusting, by an artist, is the necessary and negative aspect of the impulse toward the pursuit of beauty.

> T. S. ELIOT: 'Dante', *The Sacred Wood*, 1920

. . . the essential advantage for a poet is not to have a beautiful world with which to deal: it is to be able to see beneath both beauty and ugliness; to see the boredom, the horror, and the glory.

> T. S. ELIOT: *The Use of Poetry*, 1933

F

The sensitive poet turns from ugliness seen in his surroundings. The sensitive and mature poet will look behind this ugliness, and see the beauty of which it is the distortion.

E. W. F. TOMLIN: Lectures on Modern Poetry,
delivered to the Speech Fellowship, 1936

I seem to find as I grow older that the most beautiful and most rare thing in the world is truth.

DELACROIX

What the imagination seizes as Beauty must be truth.

JOHN KEATS in a letter to Benjamin Bailey,
22 November 1817

❧ TRUTH ❧

. . . *the true Poets must be truthful.*
WILFRED OWEN, Notes for his poems

They must, it seems, tell the truth as they really see it. This is natural and not unexpected; for no artist, however fantastic, would admit that what he says has not its own kind of truth. But the moderns go further than this and stress a special kind of truth. The truth which they demand is not mere truth or ordinary truth, nor a simple avoidance of falsehood, but the whole truth in the full sense of the phrase, the truth as they see it, with their whole natures, when their wits and sensibilities and emotions are all at work.

C. M. BOWRA: *The Creative Experiment,* 1949

All poetry is difficult, almost impossible, to write; and one of the great permanent causes of error in writing poetry is the difficulty of distinguishing between what one really feels and what one would like to feel, and between the moments of genuine feeling and the moments of falsity.

T. S. ELIOT in a lecture

The modern poet, who lives in an age of psychological discovery and of an increased awareness of the subtler currents in himself, has a harder task to tell the whole truth than his ancestors in simpler and less self-conscious times. He is particularly at a disadvantage because the modern means which scientists have invented for psychology, the language which they use and their experimental approach to the subject, are unfitted for poetry. The poet does not analyse himself in this way, nor can he use an abstract language of this kind. His task is not to explain or to analyse, but to portray something just as he sees it, to catch its fleeting hues and its shifting shapes, to make us feel about it what he feels himself, even if neither he nor we are able fully to understand it. In the self modern poetry has a subject which demands the highest standards of truth as they have never been demanded before. . . .

C. M. BOWRA: *The Creative Experiment,* 1949

Truth in poetry is more than a matter of carefully stated facts. The poet does not begin with a conviction and then proceed to explain it with logical clearness. He has an impression, or a series of impressions, which he tries to understand by uncovering them in words. Nor is the result logical, though it need not offend logic. Feeling is an essential element; so is imagination. No truth is true in poetry unless it contains them. What the poet sees must be seen by the whole man before his realisation of it is true.

❊   ❊   ❊

. . . Robert Frost has said that a poem 'begins in delight and ends in wisdom'. This is true both for the poet and the reader. The poet starts to compose a poem because the joy of creation has seized him: and, as the poem takes shape, his own ideas and feelings become more clearly defined. He does not take a truth and write a poem about it. What happens is that, in the process of writing (if the poem is successful) some unguessed or dimly perceived truth grows clearer to him.

C. DAY LEWIS: *Poetry for You*, 1944

The Imagination may be compared to Adam's dream—he awoke and found it true.

JOHN KEATS: in a letter to Benjamin Bailey, 22 November 1817

. . . its object is truth . . . not standing upon external testimony, but carried alive into the heart by passion.

WILLIAM WORDSWORTH: Preface to *Lyrical Ballads*, 1802

. . . truth at a flash.

S. T. COLERIDGE

Poetry communicates ideas, but it does more. It is concerned with truth 'carried alive into the heart by passion'. It aims at the transmission through the exercise of imaginative energy, of impressions, not facts; and its words take up and absorb fresh potencies from these powerful elements in which they move. They are the same words precisely as when they occur in prose. But a new virtue (in the fine old sense of the term) has passed into them.

JOHN LIVINGSTON LOWES: *Convention and Revolt in Poetry*, 1919

Every good poem . . . is a bridge into the unknown. Science, too, is always making expeditions into the unknown. But this does not mean that science can supersede poetry. For poetry enlightens us in a different way from science; it speaks directly to our feelings or imagination. The findings of poetry are no more and no less true than science.

C. DAY LEWIS: *Poetry for You*, 1944

Science finds its knowledge of the world by mass measurement, that is by social means . . . and what it finds is never true but more and more nearly true. This holds of physics, of history, and also of psychology. . . . But I believe that there is truth which is not reached by these means. . . . The mind of man has a knowledge of truth beyond the near-truths of science and society. I believe that poetry tells this truth.

J. BRONOWSKI: *The Poet's Defence*, 1939

Poetic truth . . . must be accepted as the corollary and crown of poetic pleasure. It is not, like scientific truth, verifiable. . . . We might go, equipped with a pair of field-glasses and a textbook on ornithology, to the seas where, Shelley sang,

'The halcyons brood around the foamless isles.'

Yet it would not establish the truth of the line if we observed whole colonies of halcyons brooding there; nor would it detract from its truth if we found not a single halcyon, but a great deal of foam. . . . Poetry persuades us of its truth as irresistibly as a woman's tones and looks persuade a man that he is truly loved.

C. DAY LEWIS: *The Poetic Image*, 1947

. . . we say 'Yes, that is true, I feel with all my heart it is true.' Not scientifically true, nor logically true. But sensuously, emotionally or spiritually true.

C. DAY LEWIS: *Enjoying Poetry*, 1947

The human being lives—I mean, spiritually lives—by means of two kinds of truths, scientific truth and poetic truth. And you cannot live, though in Victorian times some people thought you could, by either of these alone. Poetic truth does not pretend to be objective, but then does any human being in his more human moments? In ordinary conversation we do not usually set out to give an accurate account of objects or events; we are usually concerned to put over our own reaction to something. And this is exactly what the poet does; but he does it as a specialist. Poetry, in fact, is a precision instrument for recording a man's reactions to life. And I cannot foresee a time when we shall not need such an instrument.

LOUIS MACNEICE: 'English Poetry Today',
The Listener, 2 September 1948

So far as any single function of spiritual life can be said to have an intrinsic value, poetry, it seems to me, possesses it just as other functions do, and it is in each case irreplaceable. And further, it seems to me, poetry attains its own aim, and in doing so makes its own contribution to the whole, most surely and fully when it seeks its own end without attempting to reach those of co-ordinate functions, such as the attainment of philosophic truths or the furtherance of moral progress. But then I believe this because I also believe that the unity of human nature in its diverse activities is so intimate and persuasive that no influence can affect any one of them alone, and that no one of them can operate or change without transmitting its influence to the rest. If I may use the language of paradox, I would say that the pursuit of poetry for its own sake is the pursuit both of truth and goodness. Devotion to it is devotion to 'the good cause of the world'; and wherever the imagination is satisfied, there, if we had a knowledge we have not, we should discover not idle fancy, but the image of a truth.

A. C. BRADLEY: *Oxford Lectures on Poetry*, 1909

❧ EXPERIENCE ❧

Poetry can communicate the actual quality of experience with
a subtlety and precision approachable by no other means.
F. R. LEAVIS, *New Bearings in English Poetry*

We have seen that it is not the subject matter which makes a poem, but
the way this matter is regarded by the poet. Nor is it truth or beauty
in any philosophical sense, but rather the way the poet has assimilated
these and made them an inseparable part of his work. It follows, then,
that the experience which gives rise to a poem cannot be judged by
any journalistic standard of 'news value'. It is the quality of the
experience that counts—or, rather, the quality of the mind that meets
the experience.

◉   ◉   ◉

Men without imagination or sensitiveness can live through a lifetime
of wonderful adventures, and at the end they are as poor as when they
started; whereas a man of fine imaginings could, like Hamlet, 'be
bounded in a nutshell yet count himself a king of infinite space'. In the
same way, an unseeing peasant could live four-score years in the
changing beauties of an English countryside, and yet be less profited
by it than Keats was by a walk on Hampstead Heath.

P. H. B. LYON: *The Discovery of Poetry*, 1930

◉   ◉   ◉

J. C. Squire tells of a cabin-boy who accompanied the Ancient Mariner
on his voyage. Questioned on his return, he said that there was a lot of
ice about, but later they couldn't get enough to drink.

◉   ◉   ◉

If your everyday life seems poor to you, do not accuse it; accuse yourself, tell yourself you are not poet enough to summon up its riches,
since for the creator there is no poverty and no poor or unimportant
place.

R. M. RILKE: *Letters to a Young Poet*, 17 February 1903

The real happenings in life are not eating and walking and going bald, and getting rich and killing your enemies; but grief, love, sympathy, fear, happiness.

P. H. B. LYON: *The Discovery of Poetry*, 1930

'I will write,' I said, 'as truly as I can from experience, actual individual experience, not from book-knowledge.' But yet it is wonderful how exactly the knowledge from good books coincides with the experience of men of the world.

S. T. COLERIDGE: *Anima Poetæ*, 17 March 1805

The Wife of Bath herself is simply Chaucer's multifarious and vivid reading of books, and his alert and omniverous reading of life, poured together *con amore* into the mould of a superbly vital imaginative conception.

JOHN LIVINGSTON LOWES: *Convention and Revolt in Poetry*, 1919

The amazing capacity of his [the poet's] for ordering speech is only a part of a more amazing capacity for ordering his experience.

I. A. RICHARDS: *Science and Poetry*, 1935

It [the poetic 'idea'] unites aspects of existence that ordinarily remain unconnected, and in this lies its value. The secret of genius is perhaps nothing else than this greater availability of all experience coupled with larger stores of experience to draw upon. The man of genius seems to take in more every minute than his duller companion, and what he has received seems to be more readily at his disposal when he needs it.

I. A. RICHARDS: *Practical Criticism*, 1929

It is equally excellent and inconclusive to say that one must write from experience. What kind of experience is intended, and where does it begin and end? Experience is never limited, and it is never complete; it is an immense sensibility, a kind of huge spiderweb, of the finest silken threads, suspended in the chamber of consciousness and catching every air-borne particle in its tissue. It is the very atmosphere of the mind; and when the mind is imaginative—much more when it happens to be that of a man of genius—it takes to itself the faintest

hints of life, it converts the very pulses of the air into revelations. . . .
The power to guess the unseen from the seen, to trace the implications
of things, to judge the whole piece by the pattern; the condition of
feeling life, in general, so completely that you are well on your way
to knowing any particular corner of it—this cluster of gifts may almost
be said to constitute experience, and they occur in country and in
town, and in the most differing stages of education. If experience
consists of impressions, it may be said that impressions *are* experience,
just as (have we not seen it?) they are the very air we breathe.

HENRY JAMES: 'The Art of Fiction', *Partial Portraits*, 1888

I think of experience as acting, not upon, but in and with the poet—I
conceive the poet, not as having, but as being, his experience.

H. W. GARROD: *Poetry and the Criticism of Life*, 1931

The world of the poet must be a continuation of the world of ordinary
human experience.

J. MIDDLETON MURRY

There is plenty of connection between life and poetry, but it is, so to
say, a connection underground. The two may be called different forms
of the same thing: one of them having (in the usual sense) reality, but
seldom fully satisfying imagination; while the other offers something
which satisfies imagination but has not full 'reality'. . . . The one
touches us as beings occupying a given position in space and time, and
having feelings, desires, and purposes due to that position: it appeals to
imagination, but appeals to much besides. What meets us in poetry has
not a position in the same series of time and space, or, if it has or had
such a position, it is taken apart from much that belonged to it there;
and therefore it makes no direct appeal to those feelings, desires and
purposes, but speaks only to contemplative imagination—imagination
the reverse of empty or emotionless, imagination saturated with the
results of 'real' experience, but still contemplative.

A. C. BRADLEY: 'Poetry for Poetry's Sake',
Oxford Lectures on Poetry, 1909

❋   ❋   ❋

And yet—this is overlooked in our popular conception of the poet as an absent-minded dreamer—he is well aware of the 'real' world. When he chooses, he can observe it with such vividness that the reader's senses may react more excitedly than to the world itself. But the poet's eye has more than sight: it has insight. It both sees and penetrates.

✽ OBSERVATION ✽

He, the trained spy.
W. H. AUDEN

Active and prompt to see, and to enjoy
Because he sees.
WILLIAM WORDSWORTH: Notebook for *The Prelude*

True imagination is based always on observation; it is a summary of
the evidence of the senses, intensified in the memory, and carried
forward one stage into the future where it stands as a revelation of a
truth not yet achieved by the slower processes of nature. False imagination is simply a wilful distortion of the evidence of the senses.

KEITH VAUGHAN in *Penguin New Writing*

He stood and watched the cobbler at his trade,
The man who slices lemons into drink,
The coffee-roaster's brazier, and the boys
That volunteer to help him turn its winch.
He glanced o'er books on stalls with half an eye,
And fly-leaf ballads on the vendor's string,
And broad-edge gold-print posters by the wall.
He took such cognizance of men and things,
If any beat a horse, you felt he saw;
If any cursed a woman, he took note. . . .

ROBERT BROWNING: 'How it Strikes a
Contemporary', 1855

Nothing escaped him. His perceptive power, for combined speed and
accuracy of working, is incredible. His mind was like a sensitive plate
which took instantaneously the impression of anything that passed
within its range, and stored up its records with no conscious effort.

J. W. MACKAIL: *An Approach to Shakespeare*, 1930

His feet are firmly set upon 'this goodly frame the earth', his eyes are focussed on the daily life around him, and he misses no tiny detail of a bird's flight, a flower's growth, a housewife's task, or the emotions written on a human face.

CAROLINE SPURGEON: *Shakespeare's Imagery*, 1935

When the Present has latched its postern behind my
    tremulous stay,
And the May month flaps its glad green leaves like wings
Delicate-filmed as new-spun silk, will the neighbours say
'He was a man who used to notice such things'?

THOMAS HARDY: 'Afterwards', *Collected Poems*, 1919

Poetic creation, what is this but seeing the thing sufficiently? The *word* that will describe the thing follows of itself from such clear intense sight of the thing.

THOMAS CARLYLE

Try to be one of the people on whom nothing is lost.

HENRY JAMES

Rodin helped Rilke to see things. 'What he sees and surrounds with sight is always to him the only thing, the world in which everything is happening; when he moulds a hand, it is alone in space, and nothing exists but a hand; and God in six days made only a hand and poured out the waters round it and arched the heavens above it; and rested upon it when all was completed, and there was a glory and a hand.'

Memoirs of Rodin: Lou Andreas-Salomé

Examine nature accurately, but write from recollection; and trust more to your imagination than to your memory.

S. T. COLERIDGE: *Table Talk*, 22 September 1830

❧ PRECISION ❧

Vagueness is half a lie.

He was a poet and hated the approximate.

R. M. RILKE: The Notebook of Malte Laurids Brigge

. . . the sensibility to detail and the power of precise statement which we welcome in all great poets, and miss when Shelley or Swinburne denies them to us.

Reviewer in The Times Literary Supplement

His business is communication through language; when he is an imaginative writer, he is engaged in the most difficult form of communication, where precision is of the utmost importance, a precision which cannot be given beforehand but has to be found in every new phrase.

T. S. ELIOT: 'The Classics and the Man of Letters', 1942

It's only the second-rate poets, or the first-rate in their second-rate moments, who allow themselves to generalize and to describe things hazily.

Author Unknown

Cut out all those pages about moonlight. . . . Show us the moon's reflection in a piece of broken glass.

ANTON CHEKHOV in a letter to a young writer

. . . the only technique that matters is that which compels words to express an intensely personal way of feeling, so that the reader responds, not in a general way that he knows beforehand to be 'poetical', but in a precise particular way. . . .

F. R. LEAVIS: New Bearings in English Poetry, 1932

The desire to express experience exactly is extremely important to modern poets, and they see what it demands of them. So far from being careless or reckless in their art, they have an ideal of exactness and precision. So Eliot stresses the need to get every word right:

> The common word exact without vulgarity,
> The formal word precise but not pedantic,
> The complete consort dancing together.

                    C. M. BOWRA: *The Creative Experiment*, 1949

Out of the slimy mud of words, out of the sleet and hail of verbal imprecisions,
Approximate thoughts and feelings, words that have taken the place of thoughts and feelings,
There spring the perfect order of speech, and the beauty of incantation.

                    T. S. ELIOT: *Four Quartets*, 1944

... This precision is of a special kind. It is not logical or intellectual. It does not mean that everything which the poet says must be reduced to ordinary categories of thought and pruned of all wild or illogical elements. It is an ideal of truth to emotion, to all that the poet feels, to those darker states of mind bordering on the unconscious which he does not fully understand but knows to be important in his whole condition. Poets try to present complex states with a faithful regard for their emotional and imaginative significance. They must do more than convey ideas: they must re-create certain states for their readers as they have themselves known them.

                    C. M. BOWRA: *The Creative Experiment*, 1949

                    ⊛   ⊛   ⊛

The precision poets seek is not the exactness of the foot-rule. It is the precision that comes when we observe with intuition as well as with reason, when we know the letter to be valueless except as a symbol of the spirit.

✣ THE LETTER AND ✣
THE SPIRIT

Poet: *O cuckoo, shall I call thee bird,*
            Or but a wandering voice?
Examiner: *State the alternative preferred:*
            Give reasons for your choice.
                A. E. HOUSMAN

. . . There are very many people who, if they read any poetry at all, try
to take all its statements seriously—and find them silly. 'My soul is a
ship in full sail', for example, seems to them a very profitless kind of
contribution to psychology.   I. A. RICHARDS: *Practical Criticism*, 1929

A Scotswoman is listening to Wordsworth being read by her son:
   'It was a beauteous evening, calm and free.'
   'Weel, we a' ken there's no chairge for it,' Mrs McOrmick admitted.
   The reader went on with, 'The holy time is quiet as a nun, breath-
less with adoration.'
   'It's a peety,' Mrs McOrmick commented with some severity, 'he
couldna appreciate the weather without being Popish about it.'
                    Told by E. C. BENTLEY

We think it is impossible that anyone could read Keats' line about
'sweet-peas on tiptoe for a flight' and have no image of the sweet-pea,
but a scientist of the deepest dye thinks it foolish to talk of a sweet-pea
being on tiptoe for a flight, an incomprehensible or a stupid way of
talking. On being asked to admit the bare accuracy of this description,
one of them replies: 'No, I can *not* see how a sweet-pea looks like
that.' After further explanations he admits that the shape of a sweet-
pea resembles that of a restless butterfly, but objects that its stalk is an
essential part of the sweet-pea; in short, a sweet-pea is not a butterfly,
so why talk as if it were?

      KATHARINE M. WILSON: *Sound and Meaning*
                            in English Poetry, 1930

The lines from Tennyson:

> Alone and warming his five wits
> The white owl in the belfry sits

struck, one may recall, Yeats' literal-minded acquaintance as 'the observation of a lunatic'. So with Omar Khayyam's 'I came like water and like wind I go'.

'What is the meaning of that?' he enquired. 'How is that possible—
"I came like water and like wind I go"?'

JOHN HALL WHEELOCK: *Poets of Today*, 1954

True poetry . . . is not, as some suppose, a kind of verbal confectionery, with cramp fantastic laws that impose great labour to little purpose. 'If one has anything to express in words, why go thus round-about?' asks our sternly prosaic friend. The relations of the human mind with the world are not so simple as he takes for granted. Men are not only intellectual and moral, but emotional and imaginative. Sorrow and joy are very real, yet often very illogical; and so also, and oftener, are those faint rapid shadows and gleams that pass continually over the mind, composing the multiplex hue of life. The moods of the sagest— are they never submissive to the wind in a keyhole, the crackling of the flame, a vernal odour, or the casual brightness or gloom upon a landscape?

WILLIAM ALLINGHAM

I totally differ from your idea that the Mariner should have had a character and a profession. . . .

CHARLES LAMB in a letter to Wordsworth

One evening riding near Rydal I saw Wordsworth sauntering towards me, wearing a shade over his eyes, which were weak, and crooning out loud some lines of a poem he was composing. I stopped to avoid splashing him and apologized for having intruded upon him. He said, 'I am glad I met you, for I want to consult you about some lines I am composing in which I want to make the shadow of Etna fall across Syracuse, the mountain being forty miles from the city. Would this be possible?' I replied that there was nothing in the distance to prevent the shadow of the mountain falling across the city. The only difficulty was that Etna is exactly north of Syracuse. 'Surely,' said Wordsworth, 'it is a little N.E. or N.W.' And as he was evidently determined to make the shadow fall the way he wanted it, I did not contradict him.

G. VENABLES: quoted by Francis Kilvert in his *Diary*

Poetry is not based on opinions, which may be mistaken. Nor does its validity depend on matters of fact, which may be as false as the history in one of Keats's most famous sonnets. Granted that it can be strengthened by fact and richly coloured by beliefs, yet what nourishes the roots is emotion.

BABETTE DEUTSCH: *New York Times Book Review*

Poetry gives, not facts, but the poet's impression of facts.

JOHN LIVINGSTON LOWES

Poetry . . . has nothing to do with facts, though everything to do with truth.

GERALD BULLETT: *Readings in English Literature*, 1946

The primary fact about poetry is that fact means nothing to it. Though it seems like poetry to say so, nothing, for poetry, happens in time. . . . The experience which poetry, or the poet, *is* (*is* and not *has*) stand out of time. It is an experience, moreover, in which the distinction between expression and impression has no part.

H. W. GARROD: *Poetry and the Criticism of Life*, 1931

Shakespeare acquired more essential history from Plutarch than most men could from the whole British Museum.

T. S. ELIOT: 'Tradition and Individual Talent'

Poetry . . . is strictly the language of the imagination; and the imagination is that faculty which represents objects, not as they are in themselves, but as they are moulded, by other thoughts and feelings, into an infinite variety of shapes and combinations of power. This language is not the less true to nature because it is false in point of fact; but is much the more true and natural if it conveys the impression which the object, as it is under the influence of passion, makes on the mind.

WILLIAM HAZLITT: *Lectures on the English Poets*, 1818

Poetry starts from the actual and ends in the true—as Coleridge started from the account of 'the Citie Xandu' on the eightieth page of Purchas's Third Part, and ended in the vision of the stately pleasure-dome. . . .

JOHN LIVINGSTON LOWES: *Convention and Revolt in Poetry*, 1919
G

If the artistic medium, of whatever sort, were capable of actual reproduction, there would be no art. For the 'effects of grandeur', to use a
pregnant phrase of Meredith's, 'are wrought out through a series of
illusions, that are illusions to the sense within us only when divorced
from the groundwork of the real'. But it is that divorce which true art
never makes.

JOHN LIVINGSTON LOWES: *Convention and Revolt in Poetry*, 1919

Imagination . . . a more cunning artist than Imitation. For Imitation can
only fashion what it has seen, but Imagination what it has not seen, also;
conceiving it on the analogy of what exists.

APOLLONIUS: translated by F. L. LUCAS

You speak of Lord Byron and me—There is this great difference
between us. He describes what he sees—I describe what I imagine.
Mine is the hardest task.

JOHN KEATS in a letter to George and
Georgiana Keats, 17–27 September 1819

The poet's business is not to *describe* things to us, or to tell us about
things, but to create in our minds the very things themselves.

LASCELLES ABERCROMBIE: *Poetry: Its Music and Meaning*, 1932

The poet's re-creation includes both the object and the sensations con-
necting him with the object, both the facts and the tone of an experience: it is when object and sensation, happily married by him, breed
an image in which *both* their likenesses appear, that something 'comes
to us with an effect of revelation'.

C. DAY LEWIS: *The Poetic Image*, 1947

Shakespeare . . . was the man who of all modern, and perhaps ancient
poets, had the largest and most comprehensive soul. All the images of
nature were still present to him, and he drew them not laboriously, but
luckily; when he describes any thing, you more than see it, you feel
it too.

JOHN DRYDEN: *An Essay on Dramatic Poesy*, 1668

. . . the fine balance of truth in observing, with the imaginative faculty in modifying the objects observed.

S. T. COLERIDGE: Biographia Literaria, 1817

Verse, whether directed to the ear or to the eye, is the outward and visible sign that we are entering the world where truth of literal fact yields place to another truth.

JOHN LIVINGSTON LOWES

◉   ◉   ◉

What is it that makes the difference between the vision of the true poet, and the obtuse literalmindedness of some of his readers? It is implied by Lessing when he says that beauty is perceived, not by the eye, but by the imagination behind it. And Blake echoes him by asserting that we should look not *with* but *through* the eye. Agreed on that point, what is it, in the artist or poet, which makes him able to look at things in that way? Is it a quality of self-surrender?—the capacity to lose his personal identity and merge his spirit with that of the person or object he contemplates? Whatever it is, it causes him to see the world with love, and with that intensity of awareness that is one of the gifts of love.

❧ LOVE AND GUSTO ❧

I love everything for what it is.
COURBET, the painter

Only when a thing is grasped in the closest conceivable relationship—
the relationship of love—do we begin to know that we are penetrating
into the inner nature of that thing. Only in love can we give ourselves
out fully enough to lose ourselves and so make real both the world and
ourselves.

GEORGE WHALLEY: *Poetic Process*, 1953

My productiveness proceeds in the final analysis from the most immediate admiration of life, from the daily inexhaustible amazement at it.

R. M. RILKE: *Selected Letters*

The infinite quantity of dramatic invention in Shakespeare takes from
his *gusto*.

WILLIAM HAZLITT

The excellence of every art is its intensity. . . .

JOHN KEATS in a letter to George and
Thomas Keats, 21 December 1817

It [the poetic view of life which Brooke is trying to express] consists
in just looking at people and things as themselves—neither as useful nor
moral nor ugly nor anything else; but just as being. At least, that's a
philosophical description of it. What happens is that I suddenly feel
the extraordinary value and importance of everybody I meet, and
almost everything I see. In *things* I am moved in this way, especially by
some things; but in people by almost all people. That is, when the
mood is on me. I roam about places—yesterday I did it even in Birmingham!—and sit in trains and see the essential glory and beauty of

all the people I meet. I can watch a dirty middle-aged tradesman in a railway-carriage for hours, and love every dirty, greasy, sulky wrinkle in his weak chin and every button on his spotted unclean waistcoat. I know their states of mind are bad. But I'm so much occupied with their being there at all, that I don't have time to think of that. I tell you that a Birmingham gouty Tariff Reform fifth-rate business man is splendid and immortal and desirable.

RUPERT BROOKE in a letter to F. H. Keeling,
20–23 September, 1910

❧ 'FOR THE FIRST TIME' ❧

The man could not look out of a window without seeing
something that had never been seen before.
J. M. BARRIE on Thomas Hardy

This loving gusto is a kind of innocence. The poet is re-born into his experience, and becomes a child—though a child with the mind and accumulated resources of a man. The world he looks at still has the dews of creation on it.

⁕   ⁕   ⁕

Life is the real and most miraculous miracle of all. If one had never before seen a human hand and were suddenly presented for the first time with this strange and wonderful thing, what a miracle, what a magnificently shocking and inexplicable and mysterious thing it would be. In my plays I want to look at life—at the commonplaces of existence—as if we had just turned a corner and run into it for the first time.

CHRISTOPHER FRY: quoted in *Life* (U.S.A.)

Poetry lifts the veil from the hidden beauty of the world, and makes familiar objects be as if they were not familiar. . . .

P. B. SHELLEY

Poetry is revelation. A poem gives the world back to the maker of the poem, in all its original strangeness, the shock of its first surprise. It is capable of doing the same for the rest of us.

JOHN HALL WHEELOCK: *Poets of Today*, 1954

The lucky ones seem to be always as if they just came into the world. . . . There is still in them something of Adam upon the first day; they reconnoitre, with shining eyes, the layout of the garden, and stare in admiration at such novel curiosities as the moon and the stars.

C. E. MONTAGUE

Before the time of Shakespeare men had grown used to the Ptolemaic astronomy, and since the time of Shakespeare men have grown used to the Copernican astronomy. But poets have never grown used to the stars; and it is their business to prevent anybody else ever growing used to them. And any man who reads for the first time the words, 'Night's candles are burnt out', catches his breath.

G. K. CHESTERTON: *Chaucer*, 1932

To be with Lawrence was a kind of adventure, a voyage of discovery into newness and otherness. . . . He looked at things with the eyes, so it seemed, of a man who had been at the brink of death and to whom, as he emerges from the darkness, the world reveals itself as unfathomably beautiful and mysterious. For Lawrence, existence was one continuous convalescence; it was as though he were newly re-born from a mortal illness every day of his life.

ALDOUS HUXLEY: Introduction to
The Letters of D. H. Lawrence, 1938

The poet shares with other artists the faculty of seeing things as though for the first time. To a certain extent this faculty is merely childish wonder extended into maturer life. But it differs from mere childishness because it is combined with a vividly imagined memory of past experiences, so that while experiences can ever be re-experienced as though they were new, at the same time they can be related and compared with the past forms in which they were experienced, which still remain fresh and distinct.

STEPHEN SPENDER: *Life and the Poet*, 1942

The poet is one who carries the simplicity of childhood into the powers of manhood; who, with a soul unsubdued by habit, unshackled by custom, contemplates all things with the freshness and the wonder of a child. . . .

S. T. COLERIDGE: 8th Lecture on Shakespeare, 1811–12

Poetry is the language in which man explores his own amazement. It is the language in which he says heaven and earth in one word. It is the language in which he speaks of himself and his predicament as though for the first time.

CHRISTOPHER FRY: Broadcast talk, 'A Playwright Speaks',
The Listener, 23 February 1950

Draw near to Nature. Then try, as if you were one of the first men, to say what you see and experience and love and lose.

R. M. RILKE: Letter from Paris, 17 February 1903

I have learned to count each day
Minute by breathing minute—
Birds that lightly begin it,
Shadows muting its end—
As lovers count for luck
Their own heart-beats and believe
In the forest of time they pluck
Eternity's single leaf.

C. DAY LEWIS: 'The Poet', *Word over All*, 1943

A man is enclosed in a rocket and shot up to the moon. He is given food, oxygen, covering, warmth; all the apparatus necessary for living and dying. He is also given pen, ink and paper. He is in constant communication with the earth, to which he is every day sending back messages. Nothing which he finds on the moon corresponds to anything which has been described on the earth, either in the way of natural conditions or of accepted ideas. In order to give a true idea of the moon, he is therefore compelled to make people on the earth imagine it. At the same time he has to express the moon in terms of what they already know and feel, otherwise they would not be able to relate the experience of the moon with their own lives. . . .

This is the simplest possible account of the poet's creative activity in life. He retains throughout all the situations in life in which he is an artist the sense of being the man who lands on the moon, steps out of his rocket, and stares at the unexperienced landscape for the first time.

STEPHEN SPENDER: *Life and the Poet*, 1942

⊛   ⊛   ⊛

It is by regarding the world with an intensity of love, as though seeing it always for the first time, that the spirit is detected behind the letter, the essence extracted from the fact. So the poet's vision is something closer and warmer than observation of the thing perceived. It is an identification with it.

❧ CHARACTER AND IDENTITY ❧

Unless the soul goes out to meet what we see, we do not see
it; nothing do we see, not a beetle, not a blade of grass.
W.H. HUDSON, *The Book of the Naturalist*

Poets—the best of them—are a very chameleonic race; they take the colour not only of what they feed on but of the very leaves under which they pass.

P. B. SHELLEY

Poets stick to nothing deliberately, but let what will stick to them, like burrs when they walk in the fields.

ROBERT FROST

That limitless solitude, that regarding each day as a lifetime, that oneness with everything.

R. M. RILKE: *Letters*, 1902–6

Birds fly through us: the tree I look at is growing in me!

R. M. RILKE in his poem 'Experience'

He seemed to know, by personal experience, what it was like to be a tree or a daisy or a breaking wave or even the mysterious moon itself. He could get inside the skin of an animal and tell you in the most convincing detail how it felt and how, dimly, inhumanly, it thought.

ALDOUS HUXLEY: Introduction to
The Letters of D. H. Lawrence, 1938

. . . if a Sparrow come before my Window I take part in its existence and pick about the Gravel.

JOHN KEATS in a letter to Benjamin Bailey,
22 November 1817

Let your rhythmical sense wind itself in and out among men and women, omnibuses, sparrows—whatever come along the street— until it has strung them together in one harmonious whole. That perhaps is your task—to find the relation between things that seem incompatible yet have a mysterious affinity, to absorb every experience that comes your way fearlessly and saturate it completely so that your poem is a whole, not a fragment; to re-think human life into poetry and so give us tragedy again and comedy by means of characters not spun out at length in the novelist's way, but condensed and synthesized in the poet's way.

VIRGINIA WOOLF: *Letter to a Young Poet*, 1932

From my very childhood, I have been accustomed to abstract and, as it were, unrealize whatever of more than common interest my eyes dwelt on, and then by a sort of transfusion and transmission of my consciousness to identify myself with the object.

S. T. COLERIDGE: *Biographia Epistolaris*

Man must not be satisfied with observation, analysis, inference—he must *become* for the time being what he wants to understand.

A. R. ENTWHISTLE: *The Study of Poetry*, 1928

So that it will be the wish of the Poet to bring his feelings near to those of the persons whose feelings he describes; nay, for short spaces of time, perhaps, to let himself slip into an entire delusion, and even confound and identify his own feelings with theirs. . . .

WILLIAM WORDSWORTH: Preface to *Lyrical Ballads*, Third edition, 1802

The creation of a work of art, we will say the creation of a character in a drama, consists in the process of transfusion of the personality, or, in a deeper sense, the life, of the author into the character. This is a very different matter from the orthodox creation in one's own image.

T. S. ELIOT: Essay on Ben Jonson, *The Sacred Wood*, 1920.

Shakespeare changed as an organism changes, in response to its environment. . . . He was not impressive, for it was not his aim to impress people. He was always doing quite the reverse, taking their impressions.

J. W. MACKAIL: *Approach to Shakespeare*, 1930

Shakespeare's poetry is characterless; that is, it does not reflect the individual Shakespeare, but John Milton himself is in every line of Paradise Lost.

s. t. coleridge: *Table Talk*, 12 May 1830

He is with all his characters and feels with them all; he debates and hesitates with Hamlet, and is all impulse with Romeo; he prays to the God of battles with King Harry, and rails on Heaven with Gloucester. He was, in short, as all men of greatest imagination must be, many-sided and of many moods, not set stiffly as most of us are, running along certain well-used grooves, but almost fluid in his swift adaptability and responsiveness both to what he saw and to what he imagined.

caroline spurgeon: *Shakespeare's Imagery*, 1935

My work is that of a composite being, which happens to be signed:

goethe

This impersonal attitude—this poetic character—is in fact a kind of submission to the laws of the imagination and to its truth.

rosamond harding: *An Anatomy of Inspiration*, 1948

As to the poetical Character itself (I mean that sort of which, if I am anything, I am a Member: that sort distinguished from the wordsworthian or egotistical sublime; which is a thing per se and stands alone) it is not itself—it has no self—it is every thing and nothing—It has no character—it enjoys light and shade; it lives in gusto, be it foul or fair, high or low, rich or poor, mean or elevated—It has as much delight in conceiving an Iago as an Imogen. What shocks the virtuous philosopher, delights the chameleon Poet. It does no harm from its relish of the dark side of things any more than from its taste for the bright one; because they both end in speculation. A Poet is the most unpoetical of any thing in existence; because he has no Identity—he is continually informing and filling some other Body—the Sun, the Moon, the Sea and Men and Women who are creatures of impulse are poetical and have about them an unchangeable attribute—the poet has none; no identity—he is certainly the most unpoetical of all God's Creatures. . . . It is a wretched thing to confess; but it is a very fact that not one word I ever utter can be taken for granted as an opinion growing out of my identical nature—how can it, when I have no nature? When I am in a room with People if I ever am free from speculating on creations of my own brain, then not myself goes home to myself; but the identity of every one in the room begins to press upon me that I am in a very little time annihilated—not only among Men; it would be the same in a Nursery of children. . . .

JOHN KEATS in a letter to Richard Woodhouse,
27 October 1818

⊛   ⊛   ⊛

This famous passage, however, should be compared with another written to George and Georgiana Keats in May 1819. Although the two letters are little more than six months apart, this represents a long thought-span in that concentrated life. 'There may be intelligences or sparks of divinity in millions', he says in the second letter, 'but they are not Souls till they acquire identities, till each one is personally itself.' In other words, Keats the man was disturbed at the insecurity of character resulting from the demands of Keats the poet. He needed an answer to those questions which trouble most poets in their un-creative moments: 'What am I? Where is my centre? How can I be personally myself?' No one who has studied Keats's personality through his letters can doubt that, had he lived a little longer, he would have found his answers. And they would have been answers that made life more endurable to the man without harm to the poet; they would have been acceptable to Keats on no other terms.

A poet, though he must be 'a sensitive instrument' need not be a weather-cock, 'a feather to every wind that blows'. He can possess an identity of his own before allowing it to be momentarily possessed. Otherwise he is at the mercy of circumstances, of any personality or fleeting impulse he comes in contact with. Identification may be a willed identification, a temporary loss of one's own self for the sake of the poem, a surrender from a known centre. For surrender of some kind still remains a pre-requisite of poetry. No poet can find himself in creation without losing himself. The act of poetry is an act of love.

⊛   ⊛   ⊛

The progress of an artist is a continual self-sacrifice, a continual extinction of personality.

T. S. ELIOT: 'Tradition and Individual Talent'

The great secret of morals is love; or a going out of our own nature, and an identification of ourselves with the beautiful which exists in thought, action, or person not our own. A man, to be greatly good, must imagine intensely and comprehensively; he must put himself in the place of another and of many others; the pains and pleasures of his species must become his own.

P. B. SHELLEY: *A Defence of Poetry*, 1820

Dreaming over a subject is simply the faculty of allowing the will to focus the mind passively on the subject, so that it follows the trains of thought as they arise, stopping them only when unprofitable, but in general allowing them to form and branch naturally until some useful or interesting results occur. Having learned to dream over the subject, the thinker must learn not to obtrude his own personal wishes but to follow where the truth leads him. He who wishes to express *himself* is on the wrong track: his aim should be to express beyond himself. In fact the procedure bears an analogy to the mystic way. The sinking of the personality; the retirement for the time being of the intellect from everything irrelevant; holding the intellect by the will so that it watches, but does not disturb, the natural development of the idea; merging himself into the great sea of life beyond himself in order that he may become one with it—these are the characteristics alike of mystic, seer and thinker.

ROSAMOND HARDING: *An Anatomy of Inspiration*, 1948

❧ UNITY ❧

. . . there is a dark
Inscrutable workmanship that reconciles
Discordant elements, makes them cling together
In one society.
WILLIAM WORDSWORTH, *The Prelude*

. . . that ultimate end of all human thought and human feeling, unity.

S. T. COLERIDGE

The individual can only be happy and at rest when he finds himself as part of the whole.

J. W. GOETHE: *Poetry and Truth*, 1775

❀   ❀   ❀

The act of creation produces not only a unity with the object that is being contemplated, but a unity within the poet himself. 'Out of the conflict of images,' said Dylan Thomas, 'I try to make that momentary peace, which is called a poem.' It is not that a poet's mind is necessarily more chaotic than another's: only that a desire for harmony being his predominant aim (in thought, form and feeling), he is more aware of discordances. But in creation he becomes unified. Incompatible elements within him become molten, and are made one in the matrix of the poem.

And the curious fact is this: by becoming whole himself, all things with which he has identified himself in the act of creation become unified with each other. The world, too, is made whole. This is perhaps the poet's highest task—this act, which he shares with the mystic, of reconciling opposing qualities, and insisting on life's essential oneness.

❀   ❀   ❀

The human race to be shown as one great network or tissue which quivers is every part when one point is shaken, like a spider's web if touched.

> THOMAS HARDY: Notes for *The Dynasts*, quoted in
> *The Early Life of Thomas Hardy*, 1928

The poet knows this sense of underlying unity—the unification of apparently separate elements in himself and in the world outside himself. At his creative moments he feels the oneness of creation, as if every note struck caused a sympathetic vibration in some other object, and all the dissonances of life resolved into a single harmony. Sometimes he expresses this knowledge directly, as when Francis Thompson writes:

> Turn but a stone, and start a wing

or in that amazing poem of Blake's which includes the couplet,

> The caterpillar on the leaf
> Repeats to thee thy mother's grief.

But more frequently the knowledge is implicit in simile and metaphor, which are the heart of poetry. For metaphor is not used merely to help the poet to an exact description, or to compel the reader to compare one object with another. That is only part of the truth. It is there because, in the poet's creative vision, the two elements of the metaphor *are* one. They share a common spirit.

> CLIVE SANSOM: *Poetry and Religious Experience*, 1948

The world, like Dionysus, is torn to pieces by pure intellect; but the poet is Zeus; he has swallowed the heart of the world, and he can reproduce it as a living body.

> OWEN BARFIELD: *Poetic Diction*, 1928

On one point all mystics seem to be agreed. They are vividly aware of some principle of unity underlying all the infinite variety of life. They have not reached this position through argument, reasoning, or indeed through any process of thought. Their knowledge is the result rather of spiritual experience, so powerful as to leave no room for doubt of argument.

> A. R. ENTWHISTLE: 'Mysticism in English Poetry',
> *The Study of Poetry*, 1928

When a poet's mind is perfectly equipped for its work, it is constantly amalgamating disparate experience; the ordinary man's experience is chaotic, irregular, fragmentary. The latter falls in love, or reads Spinoza, and these two experiences have nothing to do with each other, or with the noise of the typewriter or the smell of cooking; in the mind of the poet these experiences are always forming new wholes.

T. S. ELIOT: 'The Metaphysical Poets'

Idea after idea from Coleridge's reading or experience sinks into the reservoir of memory, to couple in the dark like unseen fish and produce strange hybrids that will one day leap back to the light—there to be caught and transferred, quivering with new life, to the Mariner's ocean or to the sacred stream of Kubla Khan.

F. L. LUCAS: *The Decline and Fall of the Romantic Ideal*, 1939

Arthur is always carrying a bit of chaos around with him and turning it into cosmos.

CARLYLE on Tennyson

Do you know Donne? . . . He was one of those over-metaphysical-headed men, who can find out connections between everything and anything. . . .

LEIGH HUNT: Letter to Shelley, 20 September 1819

Shakespeare's imagination is of the same plastic kind as his conception of character or passion. 'It glances from heaven to earth, from earth to heaven.' Its movement is rapid and devious. It unites the most opposite extremes. . . .

WILLIAM HAZLITT

. . . that creative deep, which is peculiar to the poet only in degree. . . . The 'deep well of unconscious cerebration' underlies your conscious-ness and mine, but in the case of genius its waters are possessed of a peculiar potency. Images and impressions converge and blend even in the sleepy drench of our forgetful pools; but the inscrutable energy of genius which we call creative owes its secret virtue at least in part to the enhanced and almost incredible facility with which, in the wonder-working depths of the unconscious, the fragments which sink inces-santly below the surface fuse and assimilate and coalesce.

JOHN LIVINGSTON LOWES: *The Road to Xanadu*, 1930

... the poet brings into harmony, out of the welter of life, experiences which might have seemed unrelated, but which grow together through the activity of his mind and are transformed through the medium of words.

G. ROSTREVOR HAMILTON: 'The Meaning of
Tradition', *The Tell-Tale Article*, 1949

There is a most remarkable weight and unanimity of evidence, both in the verse and the critical writings of English poets, that poetry's truth comes from the perception of a unity underlying and relating all phenomena, and that poetry's task is the perpetual discovery, through its imaging, metaphor-making faculty, of new relationships within this pattern, and the rediscovery and renovation of old ones.

C. DAY LEWIS: *The Poetic Image*, 1947

To the poet alone belongs the art of depicting with negative traits, and by mixing them with positive to bring two images into one.

GOTTHOLT LESSING: *Laöcoon: The Limits of
Painting and Poetry*, 1766

Creative imagination in its fullest and finest range is a marriage of opposites.

HUGH I'ANSON FAUSSET: *Poets and Pundits*, 1947

Poetry turns all things to loveliness . . . it marries exultation and horror, grief and pleasure, eternity and change; it subdues to union, under its light yoke, all irreconcilable things.

P. B. SHELLEY: *A Defence of Poetry*, 1820

Inspiration, according to many poets, creates a state in which they see as a whole what normally they see only in fragments as parts of a temporal process; and are able to grasp from outside in the full pattern of its movement what normally they know only from the inside in separate and limited stages of development.

C. M. BOWRA: *Inspiration and Poetry*, 1951

The task of the poet is now, as always, to reveal the singleness of life beneath the nightmare of phenomena.

STEPHEN SPENDER

H

At its greatest, the imagination girdles the earth with a chain of related images, creating a new world in the image of the old. In this it is akin to the Word making darkness light; to that lovely persuasion creating order and form out of chaos—statements that are themselves merely images of an underlying unity.

DAVID CAMPBELL in *The Bulletin*, Sydney, 14 May 1952

The Imagination modifies images, and gives unity to variety; it sees all things in one. . . .

S. T. COLERIDGE: *Table Talk*, 23 June 1834

Imagination sees all things in one. It reveals itself in a balance or reconcilement of opposite or discordant qualities.

S. T. COLERIDGE

Imagination is the faculty which grasps these invisible links which bind together the visible parts of the universe.

C. DAY LEWIS

I incline to believe that analogy—likeness between dissimilar things— which is the fact underlying the possibility and reality of metaphor, holds within itself the very secret of the universe.

CAROLINE SPURGEON: *Shakespeare's Imagery*, 1935

The reconciliation of discordant elements is one of the chief tasks which poetry sets before itself in mutations kindred to those which the mere business of life imposes, more or less effectively, upon us. The 'use' of poetry, if the word were not misleading, is that its harmony can induce harmony.

CHARLES WILLIAMS: *Reason and Beauty*
in the Poetic Mind, 1933

'The excellence of every art,' said Keats, 'is . . .' What a wonderful beginning of a sentence! If the page of Keats's manuscript had ended there and the next page been lost, the world would have been breathless to know how the sentence continued. 'The excellence of every art', said Keats, 'is . . .' and he did not say that it was in its subject or in its treatment, still less that it was in its social passion or its adherence to any ethical system or in its contemporaneousness. 'The excellence of every art,' said Keats, 'is its intensity.' And what did he mean by that? Fortunately he tells us. 'Capable,' he continues, 'of making all disagreeables evaporate from their being in close relationship with Beauty and Truth.' Do not misunderstand him. By 'disagreeables' he does not mean things that are unpleasant to us; he means those things which do not agree together, which clash in our immediate experience, but which harmonize when seen in the aspect of eternity. Keats's 'disagreeables' are what I have called our incongruities, of time, of place, of individuality, of right seemingly opposed to right, of loyalty conflicting with loyalty. It is the function of art by its intensity to penetrate these incongruities, to perceive some aspect of order in the chaos of living, some aspect of beauty in that order, some aspect of truth in that beauty, and so to distil experience that we are made partakers of its essence and are enabled to re-imagine it and to renew ourselves.

CHARLES MORGAN: 'The Artist in the Community',
Liberties of the Mind, 1951

I will conclude with the words of Bishop Jeremy Taylor: 'He to whom all things are one, who draweth all things to one, and seeth all things in one, may enjoy true peace and rest of spirit.'[1]

S. T. COLERIDGE: *Biographia Literaria*, 1817

[1] *Via Pacis.*

❧ METAPHOR ❧

*The greatest thing by far is to have command of metaphor
. . . It is the mark of genius.*

ARISTOTLE

Metaphor is the expression of that unity which imagination sees in the world it looks on, when it looks with love.

◉   ◉   ◉

In prose . . . metaphor may be an explanatory, elucidatory and rationalistic element, for in prose man reasons about himself and the world. In poetry, as naturally as in a child or a lover, it springs from emotion, from feeling. Far from being a mere ornament or floriation, a flutter of fancy, or an ingenious flourish, it is a rich imaginative exercise of the whole poetic mind in contemplation of that complexity in unity which is alike the delight, the wonder and the mystery of all human experience in the world. All things bear an intrinsic resemblance to one another, since all are compounded of the same elements; and metaphor is the revelation of such resemblances.

WALTER DE LA MARE: 'Metaphor',
Private View, 1953

Their language [the poets'] is vitally metaphorical; that is, it marks the before-unapprehended relations of things, and perpetuates their apprehension.

P. B. SHELLEY: *A Defence of Poetry*, 1820

Poetry . . . is the primary activity of the human mind. Man, before he has arrived at the stage of forming universals, forms imaginary ideas. Before he reflects with a clear mind, he apprehends with faculties confused and disturbed: before he can articulate, he sings: before speaking in prose, he speaks in verse: before using technical terms,

he uses metaphors, and the metaphorical use of words is as natural to
him as that which we call 'natural'.

HERBERT READ, quoted in *The Poetic Image*, 1947

The spring of poetic thought is the imagination. And it is one of the
mysteries of the imagination that, in its working, like is attracted to
like, and new kinships are uncovered in the seemingly unlike by the
use of metaphor and simile. The imagination, in fact, seeks to simplify,
to bring to order. . . . The imagination is an active force; by bringing
together it creates something new, it creates images. The shock of their
coupling is the poetic experience.

DAVID CAMPBELL in *The Bulletin*, Sydney, 14 May 1952

The infinite variety of pleasure and pain can no more be expressed
directly by words than the endless play of light and colour on the sea.
Words do not love, hate, suffer, enjoy, any more than they taste, or
smell, or are soft or cool; they have not in themselves passion, as they
have not solidity or line. Yet, if I am a poet, they are my only medium.
What is my way out? . . . To put my feelings into words, no less than
to record my impressions of sensuous things, I must relate them to
something else. The basic convention of imagery, then, has its roots
in the essential limitations of the poet's medium; in the fact that
language itself stands in no immediate relation to the objects which it
represents. . . .

JOHN LIVINGSTON LOWES: *Convention and Revolt in Poetry*, 1919

Try to be precise and you are bound to be metaphorical.

J. MIDDLETON MURRY

This quality of precision, of clerity, of definition, is one of the vital
contributions which imagery makes to poetry. Without imagery
poetry would be abstract; and it would lack those qualities which raise
it above clear, logical expression. It is imagery which vitalizes such
expression, infusing it with copious suggestions of weights, buoyances,
textures, sounds, movements, shapes and colours. But there is, too, an
awakening of emotion, without which an experience would be dead,
and also a directing of emotion, without which the experience would
be warped, confused, and unshapely.

P. GURREY: *The Appreciation of Poetry*, 1935

We are clear and logical at the cost of being superficial or inexact. The poet more exactingly seeks absolute precision of language and thought, and the exigencies of this precision demand that he should exceed the limits of customary expression and therefore invent—sometimes words, more frequently new uses of words, most frequently phrases and figures of speech which reanimate words, and among these, above all, *metaphor*. Metaphor, in fact, for such a poet becomes the normal mode of expression.

HERBERT READ: 'Obscurity in Poetry' in
Collected Essays, 1938

Men do not *invent* those mysterious relations between separate external objects, and between objects and feelings, which it is the function of poetry to reveal. These relations exist independently, not indeed of Thought, but of any individual thinker. . . . The language of primitive men reports them as direct perceptual experience. The speaker has perceived a unity, and is not therefore himself conscious of *relation*. But we, in the development of consciousness, have lost the power to see this one as one. Our sophistication, like Odin's, has cost us an eye; and now it is the language of poets, in so far as they create true metaphors, which must *restore* this unity conceptually, after it has been lost from perception. Thus, the 'before-unapprehended' relationships of which Shelley spoke, are in a sense 'forgotten' relationships. For though they were never yet apprehended, they were at one time seen. And imagination can see them again.

OWEN BARFIELD: *Poetic Diction*, 1928

The mind of poetry is a metaphorical mind. It is unable to apprehend a phenomenon *per se*. It must see it twice—both in terms of itself and in terms of its non-self; it must see it both as what it superficially and evidently is, and also as something else that it metaphorically, but no less truly, is. The phenomenon so seen is not thus falsified; on the contrary, it is clarified and realized; it is enhanced and perhaps even explained; it is illumined by the light of another world and translated to the dimension of that world.

R. H. WARD: 'The Mind of Poetry', *The Aryan Path*

Seeking for material in which to incarnate its last inspiration, imagination seizes on a suitable word or phrase, uses it as a metaphor, and so creates a meaning. The progress is from Meaning, through inspiration to imagination, and from imagination, through metaphor, to meaning; inspiration grasping the hitherto unapprehended, and imagination relating it to the already known.

OWEN BARFIELD: *Poetic Diction*, 1928

Poetry is a double vision. With one eye it sees all that crosses before it, with a focussed clarity—unique, Eden-new—each thing valuable and astonishing in itself. With the other it sees the unseen relationships between things, the unity and continuity of existence. The merging of these two angles of sight is what constitutes poetic vision; and the expression of it, in words so ordered and dynamic that the reader's thought and feeling and imagination are stirred to share that vision, constitutes poetry.

CLIVE SANSOM in a discarded essay

At its highest, imagery, by drawing together widely separated objects and experiences into a brief and unlaboured expression, asserts the unity of human life. The poet, though often not consciously, is affirming that behind all the conflict of contrasting appearances there is a single life of the spirit. Metaphor is the applied metaphysics of poetry. Imagery in its purest form is mysticism made manifest from sources that depend on ordinary experience. It may well be that it is typical of English genius that it has discovered this way of making empiricism transcendental.

B. IFOR EVANS: *English Literature*, 1944

❧ INSPIRATION ❧

. . . this striding edge,
This hare-bell height of calm
Where intuitions swarm
Like nesting gulls, and knowledge
Is free as the winds that blow. . . .

C. DAY LEWIS, 'The Poet'

That undisturbed, direct manner of working, almost like a sleep-walker, which alone can lead to greatness. . . .

J. W. GOETHE

. . . that state of nascent existence in the twilight of imagination and just on the vestibule of consciousness.

S. T. COLERIDGE

Neither dreams nor the complete illusions of hypnosis, but just on the moonlit verge of them—the wakeful lethargy in which a creak of the floor seems an earthquake, and things with the special values of unreality acquire all the vividness of the real. . . .

MAX EASTMAN: *Enjoyment of Poetry,* 1951

It is the common experience of men of genius that their noblest 'thoughts', their keenest intuitions, seem to flash into the mind from without rather than to spring up from within. They seem to proceed from some independent agency external to mind and yet at home in it. . . .

FREDERICK GREENWOOD: *Imagination in Dreams,* 1894

Poetry . . . is something that happens when words are so used as to communicate an aspect or nuance of reality otherwise incommunicable. The operative word is 'happens'. I say poetry happens, because in the last analysis it is an event beyond the poet's conscious contriving.

The chances are that but for his disciplined skill, his command of
language, and above all his self-dedication to the arduous business of
meditation, it would *not* happen; but when it does it is something
given, something that comes by grace.

GERALD BULLETT: *The English Mystics,* 1950

The word inspiration need cause no difficulty. I mean by it a mood of
great, abnormal in fact, mental acuteness, either energetic or receptive,
according as the thoughts which arise in it seem generated by a stress
and action of the brain, or to strike into it unasked. This mood arises
from various causes. . . . All that is needful to mark is that the poetry
of inspiration can only be written in this mood of mind, even if it only
last a minute, by poets themselves. Everybody of course has like moods,
but not being poets what they then produce is not poetry.

GERARD MANLEY HOPKINS: Letter to Baillie, 10 September 1864
Further Letters of G. M. Hopkins

In these rare but sublime moments time and space disappear; the work
thus created has no limits, or, if it has, the poet does not see them. His
thought embraces and penetrates him at so great a depth that for a
moment he is set free from the conditions of the human lot. . . . It
does not last long, but nothing can take its place when it is over. It
gives to a work of poetry that primitive swing, that unlimited movement which is necessary to it; for it must have begun by being too vast
in the soul of the poet, in order, afterwards, to be great enough in
the eyes of other men.

EDMOND ARNOULD, quoted by Henri Bremond,
Prayer and Poetry

Poetry is not like reasoning, a power to be exerted according to the
determination of the will. A man cannot say, 'I will compose poetry'.
The greatest poet even cannot say it; for the mind in creation is as a
fading coal, which some invisible influence, like an inconstant wind,
awakens to transitory brightness; this power arises from within, like
the colour of a flower which fades and changes as it is developed, and
the conscious portions of our nature are unprophetic either of its
approach or its departure. Could this influence be durable in its original
purity and force, it is impossible to predict the greatness of the results;
but when composition begins, inspiration is already on the decline, and
the most glorious poetry that has ever been communicated to the

world is probably a feeble shadow of the original conceptions of the
poet.

P. B. SHELLEY: *A Defence of Poetry*, 1820

Having drunk a pint of beer at luncheon—beer is a sedative to the
brain, and my afternoons are the least intellectual portion of my life—
I would go out for a walk of two or three hours. As I went along,
thinking of nothing in particular, only looking at things around me
and following the progress of the seasons, there would flow into my
mind, with sudden and unaccountable emotion, sometimes a line or two
of verse, sometimes a whole stanza at once, accompanied, not preceded, by a vague notion of the poem which they were destined to
form part of. Then there would usually be a lull of an hour or so, then
perhaps the spring would bubble up again.

A. E. HOUSMAN: *The Name and Nature of Poetry*, 1933

❀   ❀   ❀

The ritual of creation is probably different for every poet, and for the
same poet at different times—Housman's beer, Schiller's rotten apples,
Wordsworth's walking, Shelley's boating. Dr Rosamund Harding has
made a most interesting collection of these peculiarities in her *Anatomy
of Inspiration*;[1] but so far as it concerns literature, the book is open to
two criticisms. First, insufficient distinction has been drawn between
the creative writer and the hack; between the writer who uses imagination and invention, and the one who uses only invention. And secondly,
it does not distinguish between the unpremeditated lyric, which may
be brief enough to complete itself before the coals of inspiration start
fading, and a long-planned work, such as an epic or verse drama, which
requires the sustaining power of the will. However, one can hardly
blame Dr Harding for this, because the poet himself is often uncertain
where inspiration ends and a 'desire to write' begins. Should the Muse
be left sleeping, or can she be prodded so subtly that she thinks she
wakes herself?

❀   ❀   ❀

'I believe that what determines great poetry is how far down it goes.

Woman, when I behold thee, flippant, vain,
Inconstant, childish, proud and full of fancies,
Without that modest softening that enhances

[1] Heffer, Cambridge, Revised edition 1951.

The downcast eye, repentant of the pain
That its mild light creates to heal again:
E'en then, elate, my spirit leaps and prances,
E'en then my soul with exultation dances. . . .

That hasn't much depth, has it? That's pretty awful, isn't it?'
'Of course.'
'It's Keats, all the same. But—

. . . Dying off
As if the ebbing air had but one wave.

Isn't that of an unfathomable depth, timeless, *independent* of all cir-
cumstance, schools, fashions, years, sickness, quarrels? —— hasn't been
touched as yet by *that* divinity.'

> ALFRED NOYES, discussing poetry with Hugh Wal-
> pole in the Protestant Cemetery, Rome, 1939.
> *Roman Fountain*

. . I have come to this resolution—never to write for the sake of
writing, or making a poem, but from running over with any little
knowledge or experience which many years of reflection may perhaps
give me; otherwise I will be dumb.

> JOHN KEATS in a letter to Benjamin Haydon, 8 March 1819

. . . if poetry comes not as naturally as the Leaves to a tree it had
better not come at all.

> JOHN KEATS to John Taylor, 27 February 1818

I must wait for the ringing in the silence, and I know that if I force
the ringing, then it really won't come.

> R. M. RILKE: *Selected Letters*, translated by R. F. C. Hull

A poem is not written by the man who says: I will sit down and write
a poem; but rather by the man who, captured by rather than capturing
an impulse, hears a tune which he does not recognize, or sees a sight
which he does not remember, in some 'close corner of his brain',
and exerts the only energy at his disposal in recording it faithfully.

> ARTHUR SYMONS: Introduction to *William Blake*, 1907

James Stephens once said: 'I never sit down and say to myself, "Now I am going to write a poem." No, what happens is this. A poem takes me by the scruff of the neck and says, "Sit down and write me, And see that you write me well, or else I'll knock your block off!"'

W. R. RODGERS in a broadcast, B.B.C., May 1954

Poems and Hums aren't things that you get. They are things that get you. All you can do is to go where they can get you.

A. A. MILNE: Pooh Bear in *Winnie-the-Pooh*

A good poet is someone who manages, in a lifetime of standing out in thunderstorms, to be struck by lightning five or six times; a dozen or two dozen times and he is great.

RANDALL JARRELL: *Poetry and the Age*, 1955

It wasn't on the whole my way, as a poet, to strive after the embodiment of something abstract. I received within myself impressions— impressions of a hundred sorts, sensuous, lively, lovely, many-hued— as an alert imaginative energy presented them. And I had as a poet nothing else to do but mould and fashion within me such observations and impressions, and through a vivid representation to bring it about that others should receive the same impression, when what I had written was read or heard.

J. W. GOETHE, quoted in *Convention and Revolt in Poetry*

Poetry is a distinct faculty—it won't come when called—you may as well whistle for a wind.

BYRON, quoted by E. J. Trelawny,
Records of Shelley, Byron and the Author, 1878

Now the Poet's way of apprehending the Universal is . . . by keeping true to himself, attending to his soul's inner harmony, and listening, waiting, brooding with a 'wise passiveness' until the moment when his and the larger harmony fall into tune together. The Psalmist describes the process accurately: 'While I was thus musing, the fire kindled, and at the last I spoke with my tongue.'

A. QUILLER-COUCH: Essay on 'Poetry'

In two excitingly impassioned days, when I was thinking of settling down to something else, these sonnets were given me. [The 'Orpheus' sonnets].

R. M. RILKE in a letter to Gertrud Ouckama Knoop,
February 1922

Do you agree that poetry is a 'state of mind'? I mean by that—when the mood is on, almost anything (however banal in itself) can have *poetry* written about it. When the mood is *not* on, one may write technically good stuff about the most 'poetic' theme, yet it doesn't somehow catch fire, or become memorable. It isn't poetry in the highest sense.

STEPHEN HAGGARD in a letter to Christopher Hassall,
The Timeless Quest, 1948

It acts in a divine and unapprehended manner, beyond and above consciousness.

P. B. SHELLEY

Its starting-point is some concrete suggestion, and that suggestion may be anything. It may be a stubble-field under the autumn light, that all at once touches the springs of inspiration; it may be a visit with one's sister to the River Wye, or the bugle music of the boatmen on Lake Killarney, or the nest of a fieldmouse turned up by a plough. And it may equally well be a line of Virgil, or some phrase of Horace, itself 'the birth of some chance morning or evening . . . among the Sabine hills' that in a flash gives wings to the imagination, or a page of *Purchas His Pilgrims*, or an old yellow book picked up in a Florentine bookstall.

JOHN LIVINGSTON LOWES: *Convention and Revolt in Poetry*, 1919

The poet unaccountably finds himself dominated by something which absorbs his being and excludes other interests from his mind. It is not easy to define exactly what this is, but we may mark certain elements in it. Central to it is something which may be called an idea, though in some ways it is too vague to deserve the name. It has a powerful character and atmosphere of its own, and though at first it is too indefinite for intellectual analysis, it imposes itself on the poet with the majesty and authority of vision. Even if he does not fully understand it, he feels it and almost sees it. This is usually accompanied by words which fall into rhythmical patterns, sometimes without the poet knowing what they mean. . . .

This state is not static but dynamic, a source of vivid, almost violent activity. It begins at once to shoot out ideas of great force and intensity, and these are often accompanied by words which not only clarify them and relate them to the general scheme but are themselves of an unusual force and intensity. Inspiration sets to work with a will which nothing can withstand.

In many cases an idea may move faster than the words which pursue it, and the poet is hard put to keep abreast of it. We can see evidence for this in Pushkin's manuscripts. He will often write down complete lines and variant versions of them as if trying to catch the absolutely right effect, but no less often he will leave gaps and race after the next theme which lures him on, setting down a few odd words, a phrase or a rhyme or a mere clue to what he wishes to say. The whole thing seems to have been done at an extraordinary speed, as if the inspiring thoughts were often too fast for the words which pant after them. But so lively and powerful is the source of energy, so rich in suggestions and so actively at work in his consciousness, that he is able to come back to it and fill in the gaps later by reference to it. Though few poets work with Pushkin's speed and abundance, most know something like his condition.   C. M. BOWRA: *Inspiration and Poetry*, 1951

. . . with Keats, the poem is never final, is not so much composed as *being* composed; the eye and hand are moving still.

CHARLES MORGAN: *Reflections in a Mirror*, 1944

In Shakespeare one sentence begets the next naturally; the meaning is all inwoven. He goes on kindling like a meteor through the dark atmosphere.   S. T. COLERIDGE: *Table Talk*, 7 April 1833

Shakespeare's intellectual action is wholly unlike that of Ben Jonson or Beaumont and Fletcher. The latter see the totality of a sentence or passage, and then project it entire. Shakespeare goes on creating, and evolving B out of A, and C out of B, and so on, just as a serpent moves, which makes a fulcrum of its own body, and seems for ever twisting and untwisting its own strength.

S. T. COLERIDGE: *Table Talk*, 5 March 1834.

⊙   ⊙   ⊙

When we say that a poem is inspired we mean that it gives us a sense of inevitability, as of leaves coming naturally to a tree. And there is, at the same time, an air of spontaneity. It may be only an illusion, of course—the poet may have worked intensely to achieve it—but it is there: as if the lines were being created in front of us at that very moment. We hear the poet, not only speaking, but drawing in his breath to speak. The experience and the expression are one. And about the greatest work there is this added quality—that the spontaneity is still there after a hundred readings.

❧ CONTROL ❧

. . . a good poet's made as well as born.
BEN JONSON, 'To the Memory of Master William Shakespeare'

What, in the long run, makes the poet is a sort of persistence of the emotional nature, and, joined with this, a peculiar sort of control.

EZRA POUND: *Literary Essays*, 1954

Without unceasing Practice nothing can be done. Practice is Art. If you leave off you are lost.

WILLIAM BLAKE

True ease in writing comes from art, not chance,
As those move easiest who have learned to dance.

ALEXANDER POPE: 'Essay on Criticism', 1711

The source of poetry is native and involuntary, but requires severe labour in its development.

P. B. SHELLEY in a letter to Medwin

Technique is the obstetrics of art.

E. W. F. TOMLIN

There is no art that does not demand virtuosity.

STANISLAVSKY: *My Life in Art*, 1930

A man may be born a poet, but he has to make himself an artist as well. He must master the instrument. . . .Without clarified construction and technical control, no poetical communication can be effective.

SIEGFRIED SASSOON: *On Poetry*, 1939

Organization is necessary as well as 'inspiration'. The re-creation of word and image which happens fitfully in the poetry of such a poet as Coleridge happens almost incessantly with Shakespeare. Again and again, in his use of a word, he will give a new meaning or extract a latent one; again and again the right imagery, saturated while it lay in the depths of Shakespeare's memory, will rise like Anadyomene from the sea. . . .

T. S. ELIOT: Conclusion to *The Use of Poetry*, 1933

Inspiration . . . except in very rare cases, does not dispense with effort. It simply fertilizes effort and reduces it to a minimum. Effort, however, cannot dispense with inspiration, and it is in the collaboration of both that the highest and best work is produced. Without rationalized effort and conscious control, even the inspiration of genius is liable to stray. Disordered and uncontrolled inspiration may result in fine work disfigured by want of proportion. . . .

GUSTAVE GELEY: *From the Unconscious to the Conscious* translated by Stanley de Brath, 1920

Poetry: passion and order at once.

S. T. COLERIDGE

The energy which made the poem a poem, rather than an assemblage of radiant images, was the capacity of the human brain to think through chaos, and by sheer force of the driving will behind it to impose upon confusion the clarity of an ordered whole.

JOHN LIVINGSTON LOWES: *The Road to Xanadu*, 1930

There is always in genius, I imagine, the element which Goethe, who knew whereof he spoke, was wont to designate as 'the Daemonic'. But in genius of the highest order that sudden, incalculable, and puissant energy which pours up from the hidden depths is controlled by a will which serves a vision — the vision which sees in chaos the potentiality of Form.

OHN LIVINGSTON LOWES: The same

The artist . . . must be sensitive and receptive to impressions, alert to every stimulus from within and from without, beyond the capacity of

I

ordinary men. But he must hold imperial sway over his impressions, selecting, clarifying, ordering, moulding, filing, and refiling them.

JOHN LIVINGSTON LOWES: *Convention and Revolt in Poetry*, 1919

In this process [of inspired composition] what begins by being almost unconscious becomes conscious; what is at the start an outburst of energy infused with a vague idea or an undifferentiated vision, becomes concrete and definite; what is outside the poet's control is gradually made to submit to his will and judgment. Such, or something like it, seems to be the usual experience of poets.

C. M. BOWRA: *Inspiration and Poetry*, 1951

I have twice or thrice in my life . . . tried to write as a *duty*. I can only say of the verses I then wrote that they were not good—and in poetry there is no bearing the purgatorial state of mediocrity. . . . One power however, is still left, when we adjure writing as a duty—viz., that of guiding our imaginations, as far as they will be piloted, to the particular object we wish to adopt.

THOMAS CAMPBELL in a letter to George Thomson, 1803

The artist who is not also a craftsman is no good. But, alas! most of our artists are nothing else.

J. W. GOETHE in a letter to Roderer, 1772

Mastery in poetry consists largely in the instinct for not ruining or smothering or tinkering with moments of vision.

EDMUND BLUNDEN: *Leigh Hunt*, 1930

*   *   *

'Technique' is too often regarded as a separate function from inspiration: the poet gets the original impulse, the craftsman takes over and finds words to fit. But in poetry of any worth, craftsman and poet are one. They may have had their differences in the past, but by working together at the same job they have become identified.

The apprenticeship to this craft consists of time, practice, patience and, above all, devotion. There are no substitutes. The second-rate poet can acquire certain 'tricks of the trade' which may deceive some

of his customers, just as the second-rate architect learns how to use
surface frills and decorations to disguise the poverty of his fundamental
design; but genuine craftsmanship is a growth, largely unconscious,
affecting the surface from within. It comes partly as a gift of nature,
partly from an impartial consideration of his earlier work, partly from
a loving study of that great line of English poets who have preceded
him. Their form—not their 'forms', in the sense of detachable patterns,
but form as the outward and visible sign of an inward and spiritual
meaning—has become assimilated and a craftsmanship developed
which is inseparable from the poet's vision. Technique is then an
additional cluster of brain-cells, the poet's extra sense.

❧ FORM ❧

The form of verse is not separable from the soul of poetry.

W. P. KER

The business of the poet . . . is to give order and coherence, and so freedom, to a body of experience.

I. A. RICHARDS: *Science and Poetry*, 1935

Poetry alone, through its resources of rhythm and sound, can articulate the concentrated essence of experience, and thus come closest to the universal and permanent; but it can do so only through the mastery of a concentrated form.

F. S. MATTHIESON: *The Achievement of T. S. Eliot*, 1947

To think imaginatively is the gift of genius. To give to thought, winged with imagination, an imperishable *form*—that is the supreme achievement of genius in its highest exercise.

JOHN LIVINGSTON LOWES

. . . the art of responding to the form of poetry is not less difficult than the art of grasping its content. . . .

I. A. RICHARDS: *Practical Criticism*, 1929

To attend to form in poetry is always to attend to a most important aspect of the meaning of poetry.

LASCELLES ABERCROMBIE: *Poetry: Its Music and Meaning*, 1932

There is something that eludes analysis, but which is the very heart of poetry, in the mysterious fusion of thought and form in supremely great verse.

JOHN LIVINGSTON LOWES

Form in poetry is of itself of no more value than ceremony in religion whence the spirit has departed.

A. R. ENTWHISTLE: *The Study of Poetry*, 1928

Form is not tradition. It alters from generation to generation. Artists always seek a new technique, and will continue to do so as long as their work excites them. But form of some kind is imperative. It is the surface crust of the internal harmony, it is the outward evidence of order.

E. M. FORSTER: 'Art for Art's Sake', in
Two Cheers for Democracy, 1946

. . . form does not lie simply in the correct observance of rules. It lies in the struggle of certain living material to achieve itself within a pattern.

STEPHEN SPENDER: *World within World*, 1951

To create a form is not merely to invent a shape, a rhyme or rhythm. It is also the realization of the whole appropriate content of this rhyme or rhythm. The sonnet of Shakespeare is not merely such and such a pattern, but a precise way of thinking and feeling.

T. S. ELIOT: 'The Possibility of a Poetic Drama', in
The Sacred Wood, 1920

The form is mechanic when on any given material we impress a pre-determined form, not necessarily arising out of the properties of the material—as when to a mass of wet clay we give whatever shape we wish it to retain when hardened. The organic form, on the other hand, is innate; it shapes, as it develops itself from within, and the fullness of its development is one and the same with the perfection of its outward form. Such as the life is, such is the form.

S. T. COLERIDGE: Lectures on Poetry, 1818

And this identity of content and form . . . is no accident; it is of the essence of poetry in so far as it is poetry, and of all art in so far as it is art. Just as there is in music not sound on one side and a meaning on the other, but expressive sound, and if you ask what is the meaning you can only answer by pointing to the sounds; just as in painting there is not a meaning *plus* paint, but a meaning *in* paint, or significant paint, and no man can really express the meaning in any other way than in paint and in *this* paint; so in a poem the true content and the true form neither exist nor can be imagined apart.

A. C. BRADLEY: 'Poetry for Poetry's Sake',
Oxford Lectures on Poetry, 1909

. . . a thought so passionate and alive that, like the spirit of a plant or an animal, it has an architecture of its own, and adorns nature with a new thing.

R. W. EMERSON: Essay on 'The Poet'

Technique is inseparable from its matter and . . . a poet must take care to choose a form which enables him to say exactly what he means in all its range and its subtlety.[1]

C. M. BOWRA: *The Creative Experiment*, 1949

The imagination . . . the true inward creatrix, instantly out of the chaos of elements or shattered fragments of memory, puts together some form to fit it.

S. T. COLERIDGE: *Anima Poetæ*, 1895

In its ideal, consummate moments, the end is not distinct from the means, the form from the matter, the subject from the expression; they inhere in and completely saturate each other.

WALTER PATER: *The Renaissance*, 1873

Sometimes form and content are spoken of as two separate things, as though an artist could embellish content by super-adding 'form', or concentrate on form at the expense of content. This is entirely false. Distinguishable as aspects, they are in essence inseparable. Form is itself a quality of content, and the more highly-charged the content of a statement, the more formal in character is it likely to be. To destroy the form of a line of poetry is to rob it of the most vital part of its content.

ERNEST LINDGREN: *The Art of the Film*, 1948

The principles which seem to me to delimit the existence of the poet and man of letters are *knowledge* and *form*; those both at one and the

---

[1] Or, better still, let the form choose him.

same time. The characteristic feature is that for him these two, know-ledge and form, are an organic unit, in which each determines, requires and produces the other. This unity means to him spirit, beauty, free-dom, everything.

THOMAS MANN: Broadcast Talk, 'The Artist and
Society', *The Listener*, 5 June 1952

It [imagination] sees the Free Life—the endless flux of the unfathomed sea of facts and images—but it sees also the controlling Form. And when it acts on what it sees, through the long patience of the will, the flux itself is transformed and fixed in the clarity of a realized design.

JOHN LIVINGSTON LOWES: *The Road to Xanadu*, 1930

Form, metre, rhyme—these are no more than the outer shell of the house; the important, the significant thing, is the spirit dwelling within. Pope, for example, the most admired writer of the eighteenth century, in his own manner achieved a perfect form. He built the house with a meticulous neatness and finish, he glazed it and painted it and did everything a highly skilled craftsman and decorator could do; but the house is certainly not a haunted one.

FORREST REID: *The Milk of Paradise*, 1946

When you are reading a poem, I would ask—not analysing it, and much less criticising it, but allowing it, as it proceeds, to make its full impression on you through the exertion of your re-creating imagina-tion—do you then apprehend and enjoy as one thing a certain meaning or substance, and as another thing certain articulate sounds, and do you somehow compound these two? Surely you do not, any more than you apprehend apart, when you see someone smile, those lines in the face which express a feeling, and the feeling that the lines express.

A. C. BRADLEY: *Oxford Lectures on Poetry*, 1909

❧ PRE-EXISTENCE ❧

The form often seems an inexplicable premonition of a
meaning which we have not yet grasped.

I. A. RICHARDS

It has just been said that meaning and form are one—a view not
popular with all readers and critics. The belief dear to writers of school
textbooks (and these, after all, are where most people find their
opinions on poetry) is that inspiration merely consists of the poet's
receiving an 'idea'. He is then left to decide, with the help of a book
on prosody or a useful table of metres, the rhythm that will best
express it. After that, in the same way, he works out a satisfactory
rhyme-scheme—a, b, c, d, e, f, g, etc. This settled, he is free (except for
the rhyming dictionary at his elbow) to pour his words into this
mould, remembering, of course, all that the critics have told him at
different times about the value of alliteration, onomatopœia, and so on,
so that he can toss in one of these every now and then to add to the
effect.

In practice—at least, this is my experience—the 'idea' and the form
come together. That is to say, the desire to compose (one may not
yet be fully aware of what it is about) is accompanied by an emotion
that drives its own particular rhythm. Not a 'metrical scheme', but a
unique and physical rhythm that seems to be the pulsing of an altered
heartbeat. More often than not, words are there from the start: usually
the first line or two, and frequently the last line as well. It is as if the
whole poem, form and all, already exists—whether in outer space or
inner consciousness doesn't matter. The poet's job is to collect and
bring 'down to earth' before the already fading realization of it is
dispersed again.

Craftsmanship comes in, but to help in deciding whether one's view
of the existing poem is correct, rather than to help in creating it. The
poem, in fact, is there already. All one's faculties, including craftsmanship, are concentrated on extracting it intact.

❀   ❀   ❀

He alone can conceive and compose who sees the whole at once before him.

FUSELI, the painter

Provided I am not disturbed, my subject enlarges itself, becomes methodized and defined, and the whole, though it be long, stands almost complete and finished in my mind, so that I can survey it, like a fine picture or a beautiful statue, at one glance. Nor do I hear in my imagination the parts successively, but I hear them, as it were, all at once.

W. A. MOZART: *Letters*, translated by M. M. Bozman

A poet can think his line before he knows of what words it will be made up.

J. KEARY: 'Thoughts on the Technique of Poetry',
Fortnightly Review, quoted by K. M. Wilson

Forms exist before the substance out of which they are shaped.

S. T. COLERIDGE, from Allsop's
Letters, Conversations and Recollections, 1836

I had already reached the conclusion that we are in no wise free in the presence of a work of art; that we do not create it as we please but that it pre-exists in us and we are compelled, as though it were by a law of nature, to discover it because it is at once hidden from us and necessary.

MARCEL PROUST: *Remembrance of Things Past*,
translated by C. K. Scott Moncrieff

Michelangelo always tried to conceive his figures as lying hidden in the block of marble on which he was working. The task he set himself as a sculptor was merely to remove the stone which covered them.

E. H. GOMBRICH: *The Story of Art*, 1950

So with Dante: we feel not so much that he is relating, nor that he is creating, as that he stands by, removes a veil, and shows us a truth pre-existent from all eternity and living to all eternity; a picture that impresses itself as irresistibly upon the mind as (to use his own simile) the seal impresses itself upon the wax.

G. G. COULTON: *Mediaeval Panorama*, 1938

✺ SOLITUDE AND SOCIETY ✺

*A being, like all the rest of mankind, on a planet swarming
with his fellow creatures . . . and yet a being living in an
indestructible loneliness.*
ELIZABETH DREW, *Discovering Poetry*

Again and again he must stand back from the press of habit and convention. He must keep on recapturing solitude.

WALTER DE LA MARE: *Private View,* 1953

I think if I had a free and healthy and lasting organization of heart,
and lungs as strong as an ox's so as to be able to bear unhurt the shock
of extreme thought and sensation without weariness, I could pass my
life very nearly alone, though it should last eighty years.

JOHN KEATS in a letter to John Hamilton Reynolds,
24 August 1819

What is needed is, in the end, simply this: solitude, great inner solitude. Going into yourself and meeting no one for hours on end—that is
what you must be able to attain. To be alone, as you were alone in
childhood, when the grown-ups were going about, involved with
things which seemed important and great, because the great ones
looked so busy and because you grasped nothing of their business.

R. M. RILKE: Letter from Rome, 23 December 1903,
Letters to a Young Poet, translated by Reginald Snell

What *is* this being alone, that condition we call solitude? It is a state
of many degrees, affecting both mind and spirit, of which one must
be conscious and aware, for bodily sleep however isolated is not a
condition of solitude.

We enter a room and shut the door; all other inmates of the house
being out of sight, if not out of hearing. There let us sit awhile as
motionlessly as life permits, and let us die away into ourselves and be

as passive as a glass-clear pool of water, reflecting only the mantling swans and the flowers and the trees on its margin, and the blue overhead. Leaving all comparison, all association and memories aside, let us then keep open house to all around us—these objects, as if we had never set eyes on them before, a sparrow chirping, a cock crowing, a horse's hoofs, a distant motor-horn. This is one degree of solitude.

Now let us shut our eyes and seal our ears as near as may be; and let the whole house around us, every room of it, every nook, corner and shadowy corridor, moon-lit, or by Sirius gazed upon, become a mere shadowland, silent, vacant—no sound, not even a clock's ticking, or the *wowgh* of a distant dog. All vacant, empty—and the self a mere conscious phantasm, sensible only of an irreducible minimum of physical contacts, out of that internal spangly gloom described by Keats. Then darkness and an intense awareness. This is another degree of solitude.

WALTER DE LA MARE: *Desert Islands*, 1947

No hour, however idle, in which his mind lies open and his imagination drifts, is ever wasted by an artist: only those hours are wasted which are pegged down to irrelevancies, in which he is neither writing nor lying fallow.

CHARLES MORGAN:'Fleshpots of Philistia',
The Times Literary Supplement

◉   ◉   ◉

The poet does not need leisure for the actual process of writing. Once a poem has started pushing up its shoots in his mind he can act the gardener to it at any time. It will go on growing while he is walking in the street, peeling potatoes, or talking with examination candidates. No, it is for an earlier part of the process that leisure is required: for germination.

Compared to the poet, the average person is a man of fixed character, his mind settled and opinionated. It may, of course, *unsettle* tomorrow, but no glimmering realization of this fact is allowed to ruffle today's convictions. Like Charles Lamb's universal Scot, 'He has no falterings of self-suspicion. Surmises, guesses, misgivings, half-intuitions, semi-consciousnesses, partial illuminations, dim instincts, embryo conceptions, have no place in his brain or vocabulary. . . . You cannot hover with him upon the confines of truth.' The poet, on the other hand, belongs to Lamb's 'order of imperfect intellects', because to him the intellect alone can never be enough. Intuitions, suggestions, impressions mean more to him than opinions—but they are far less manageable. He needs time and leisure, and freedom from other responsibilities, so as to hold an occasional stock-taking in the un-departmental store that is his mind. He needs to know who he is, and what (at least temporarily) he believes. He needs a period of assimilation in which the pieces of his jigsaw-consciousness can fall into place before Experience puts out a hand again to jumble them into confusion.

And leisure, in this sense, is increasingly hard to come by. The poet living a town-existence in an age of telephones, radio, cars and planes finds it much harder than a country poet of the last century, or an Elizabethan city-poet who in ten minutes could walk out of central London into wild-flowers and silence. The poet's special kind of concentration is more and more difficult to obtain. The world which should seem co-operative—an extension of the life within him—now seems antagonistic; and the happy withdrawal of an artist into himself takes on sometimes the appearance of a siege.

* * *

Today the degradation of the inner life is symbolized by the fact that the only place sacred from interruption is the private toilet.

LEWIS MUMFORD: *The Culture of Cities*, 1938

The embryonic writer [of the future] will have, not only the school-master and the captain of the games . . . for his two enemies, but the drill-sergeant, the gym-instructor, the leader of the fire squad, the Civil Defence expert, and Inspirer of the Youth Movement, and afterwards, when he grows up, the official of the Labour Exchange and the shop steward, as well as the politician and the critic. Such an existence is death to the artist; because to be able to work at his best, it is necessary for him to have an endless vista of hours and days, within the space of which he can write or paint without any interruption except those which are casual or that he makes for himself. But the modern development of 'healthy citizenship' . . . sterilizes all talent.

OSBERT SITWELL: *A Letter to My Son*, 1944

I ask myself repeatedly, with a kind of private anxiety: will it be possible for such personalities, completely devoted to the lyric art, to exist in our time, in our new forms of life, which drive men out murderously from all inner contemplation as a forest fire drives wild animals from their hidden lairs?

STEFAN ZWEIG: *The World of Yesterday*, 1943

＊ ＊ ＊

All this is true. The poet's life today is endangered, less by the obvious risks of philistinism and neglect—after all, these have been the obverse side of praise and enjoyment in every age—than by misplaced interest; by demands on his time for matters that, compared with poetry itself, are unimportant; by the insistence of society on his complete conformity and co-operation. Indeed, one can foresee a time when everyone, under a benevolent educational system, will be able to 'appreciate' poetry, at least with the intellect, and none will be left to create it.

And yet . . . Aren't we *too* ready to blame our environment?—or too willing to accept what we complain about? It would be wrong to expect the poet to be a person of 'character', in the usual sense of that word. The plastic quality of his mind is a condition of his art. But surely he can have some convictions on those matters that react upon his work. He can declare, 'The world may encroach so far and no farther'—say 'No', if necessary, to government officials and the rest, instead of meekly obeying, and protesting waspishly under his breath. After all, it was in prison that Bunyan found a very productive kind of solitude.

Every poet today—in fact, everyone with any sense of vocation— has to decide how far, for him, the demands of society may be met and turned to account, and at what point they become a menace to be skilfully avoided or passionately resisted. In other words, how the man and the artist can be reconciled. For personal happiness depends on it. The artist cannot be happy without solitude; the man cannot be happy if he feels at odds with his fellows. Successful living depends on his ability to find (for each poet there is probably a different formula) the rhythm of alternating solitude and society, leisure and activity, the inner and the outer world. And then to live with enjoyment in either world, whole-hearted, single-minded.

＊ ＊ ＊

The artist cannot isolate himself and yet he needs solitude if he is to get to the essence of art and vision, the beauty in his own spirit. Not absolute solitude, but solitude in the midst of an active, creative life.

J. W. GOETHE in a letter to W. von Humboldt, 1799

We escape the world through art, and art is our link with it.

J. W. GOETHE: *Elective Affinities*

✣ 'THE PUBLIC' ✣

*He is isolated among his contemporaries, by truth and by his
art, but with this consolation in his pursuits: that they will
draw all men sooner or later. For all men live by truth, and
stand in need of expression.*

R. W. EMERSON, Essay on 'The Poet'

This subject is very close to the last. For if the poet meets few people,
his poetry too is likely to withdraw from them and be written for
himself. But, then, even the most widely read poet writes primarily for
himself. No, that is not true either. He writes because he *has* to write,
because there is something in him that he wishes to extract whole and
imperishable, and only he can do it. But at least he does not try deliberately to reach the public. If he writes sufficiently well, the public will
in time reach him.

⊛   ⊛   ⊛

I never wrote one single Line of Poetry with the least Shadow of
public thought.

JOHN KEATS in a letter to John Hamilton Reynolds,
9 April 1818

One character belongs to all true poets, that they write from a principle within. . . .

S. T. COLERIDGE: Lectures on Poetry, 1818

The Genius of Poetry must work out its own salvation in a man: It
cannot be matured by law and precept, but by sensation and watchfulness in itself. That which is creative must create itself.

JOHN KEATS to James Hessey, 9 October 1818

So surely as an artist begins to think about what people are going to say
of his finished work, or, indeed, is consciously aware that they are

going to pass any judgment upon it at all, so surely will he, little by little, begin to put into his work something that he thinks people would like to have there.

JOHN DRINKWATER: *The Poet and Communication*,
Conway Memorial Lecture, South Place Ethical Society, 1923

Shakespeare wrote to please his audience, but first and foremost and all the time, he wrote to please himself.

J. DOVER WILSON: *The Essential Shakespeare*, 1932

Poetry is a very private matter, and is only communion with others by their merit, and by their identity with the solitary song.

JAMES STEPHENS in a broadcast talk on Chesterton

The artist is at his best when he follows his own aspirations without troubling his head about pleasing society, or, if you prefer, the public. Work done to order, or made to conform to the taste of those who have no artistic consciousness, is in danger of losing much of its value. Admittedly the state has a right, an obligation even, in these days as in those of Goethe, to turn an artist's gifts to its own service. But though the matter may be suggested, the artist must be left free to present it in his own manner, and for this reason a subject such as politics, which allows the creative faculty no free play, can only have a stultifying effect. The artist's inward life, that part of his being which is most essential, has never been so subjected to police supervision as it is now in some countries. He may have no intention whatever of involving himself in political controversy, and yet he is pressed by all sides to join in with them; his opinion is constantly being invited on all sorts of questions, many of them completely irrelevant to his art. . . .

In past days the artist used to take refuge in what was called the 'ivory tower', to live in it almost alone, his only contact with the world outside being an invisible spyglass through which he was able to distinguish the happy few capable of appreciating his work. In our day the old ivory towers have been transformed into towers of babel and are equipped with loud-speakers. This may be the reason why certain real and even important artists, like St John Perse, have retreated behind the screen of poetry which, while it is not a completely closed book, is almost beyond the reader's grasp.

JULES SUPERVIELLE in a broadcast talk,
The Listener, 12 June 1952

Up to now the writer has only pleaded the advantage to politics if he keeps his hands off: that by interfering he is likely to do more harm than good. He has not said what is at the bottom of his mind: that the creation of a work of literature is of greater importance in the long run than any political victory. 'Ivory tower' indeed! That was a wit-less sneer. It implies that the writer writes only for himself. But if he were creating something for his own sole delight, why should be bother to put it into words: why not be content with easy reverie? Why use words, the very stuff of communication, and awkward stuff to handle at that?

RICHARD HUGHES: 'The Writer's Duty',
The Listener, 22 July 1948

Just as I believe that no honest artist thinks about his audience when he is working, so do I believe that no artist who is a rational being is indifferent to the public estimation of his work when it is finished. While communication to the world beyond does not seem to be a necessity to the poet in his work, publication of his work to other people becomes a very practical and human desire once it is completed.

JOHN DRINKWATER: *The Poet and Communication*
Conway Memorial Lecture, South Place Ethical Society, 1923

Poetry may never with safety cut wholly loose from what is common to the poet and the rest of us. Subject to that, it may be as individual as it pleases. But as individuality approaches singularity it retreats from its lines of communication, and isolates itself.

JOHN LIVINGSTON LOWES

* * *

There is a halfway house between the Ministry of Propaganda and the Ivory Tower, and this is the safest address for a poet. If he ignores the public entirely he turns 'queer'. If he thinks of it exclusively he becomes a 'toady'. And neither toadiness nor queerness is a satisfactory recipe for verse. But if he goes on writing with self-respect, and yet with no feeling of disrespect for those who do not choose to read what he has written—indeed is gratefully surprised if they happen to like what he happens to offer—the chances are that he will find acceptance. Some good poets, it is true, have been temporarily ignored, but the best of every period have been generally accepted *in* that period, provided

K

they lived long enough. Even Keats, who died before he was twenty-six, had already a strong following. It may be comforting for a neglected poet to contemplate Chatterton, but there were also Chaucer and Shakespeare.

*   *   *

The greatest art, from Homer down, has had its roots deep in the common stuff. It may and will have overtones; it may and will awaken thoughts beyond the reaches of the average soul. But no attempt to make poetry once more a vital, civilizing force need ever hope to attain its goal if it sets to work solely by way of the initiates and the elect. For what the art of the coterie ignores is the weighty fact that the very public which it scouts wants in reality more than it knows it wants. The more or less crude touching of the springs of laughter and of tears, of love, and pity, and indignation, and adventure—this which it thinks is all it asks, is merely the instrument ready at the artist's hand for creating and satisfying finer needs. The Elizabethan public wanted blood and thunder; Shakespeare took the raw materials of melodrama and gave it *Hamlet*. . . . The finest and most exquisite art need make no compromise whatever with the public taste. At its height it transcends and transmutes that taste; it responds, and in its response creates.

JOHN LIVINGSTON LOWES: *Convention and Revolt in Poetry*, 1919

Because a poem can so work upon men's hearts, you have an obligation to men and to the humankind within yourself. You may sing to yourself alone, but you cannot sing for yourself alone. The poet is the only child of solitude. He should guard and cultivate his solitude. But, as he goes about his business there, he must not forget his other obligation: as he explores the labyrinth he must not lose hold of the clue.

C. DAY LEWIS: *The Poetic Image*, 1947

❧ COMMUNICATION ❧

Poets write, not to tell others, but to discover and understand
for themselves.

AUTHOR UNKNOWN

Although it is as a communicator that it is most profitable to consider
the artist, it is by no means true that he commonly looks upon himself
in this light. In the course of his work he is not as a rule deliberately
and consciously engaged in a communicative endeavour.

I. A. RICHARDS: *Principles of Literary Criticism,* 1924

We do not write in order to be understood; we write in order to
understand. But the more successfully a poem has interpreted to its
writer the meaning of his own experience, or of others' experience
which imagination has enabled him to make his own, the more
surely will it in the long run *be* understood.

C. DAY LEWIS: *The Poet's Task,* 1951

A poem does not originate out of an impulse to communicate. A poem
is what happens when a poet re-discovers, for himself, the reality we
have lost sight of, because, to use Shelley's metaphor, it has been
overlaid by the veil of familiarity.

The process, however, is not one of rediscovery and subsequent
transmital in a poem. The poem itself is part of the rediscovery. In
making it, the poet learns what it is that he has rediscovered. Thus a
child, when it begins to speak, learns what it is that it knows. And as a
child will talk to itself, with no one around to hear, so in the poem the
poet may be said to be talking to himself. He has established communication with his own being, and therefore potentially with others.

JOHN HALL WHEELOCK: *Poets of Today,* 1954

During the act of writing, the poem is an effort to express a knowledge
imperfectly felt, to articulate relationships not quite seen, to make or

discover some pattern in the world. It is a conflict with disorder, not a message from one person to another. Once the poem is written and published, however, it belongs to anyone who will take it, and the more the better.

RICHARD WILBUR: 'The Genie and the Bottle', in
Mid-Century American Poets

We may say that poetry is the communication of experience. But there is only one way for a man to communicate his experience to another, and that is to make it happen over again in the other man's mind, by rousing and controlling his imagination. Words which merely tell us *what* the experience was are not poetry: poetry consists of words which can transport the experience alive into our minds, and make it veritably *our* experience as well as the poet's.

LASCELLES ABERCROMBIE: *Poetry: Its Music and Meaning*, 1932

It is a test (a positive test, I do not assert that it is always valid negatively) that genuine poetry can communicate before it is understood.[1]

T. S. ELIOT: *Dante*, 1929

All communication depends, as Samuel Butler said, on two people: a sayer and a sayee, the speaker and the sympathetic listener. Not only must the broadcasting system be efficient, but the receiving set as well —and even then it needs to be tuned to the right station. The wavelength for poetry is imagination. If we have that, it doesn't matter much whether the poem is simple or complicated: somehow we will connect.

[1] See also 'Meaning', page 33.

✤ SIMPLICITY ✤

Simple, sensuous, passionate . . .
JOHN MILTON

The first condition, simplicity, while on the one hand it distinguishes poetry from the arduous processes of science . . . precludes, on the other hand, every affectation and morbid peculiarity.

s. t. coleridge: Lectures on Poetry, 1818

It is essential to poetry that it be simple, and appeal to the elements and primary laws of our nature.

s. t. coleridge: *The same*

Simple . . . that is to say, single in conception.

s. t. coleridge: *Table Talk*, 8 May 1824

What is simple in poetry is the unity making the poem one thing, like the unity of a picture or a statue.

w. p. ker: *Form and Style in Poetry*, 1929

I suspect that the greatest poetry *is*, as a rule, what Fitzgerald calls 'a concise and simple way of saying great things'. But all poets are not concise and simple souls, and even the simplest souls have complex moments.

JOHN LIVINGSTON LOWES

Most modern poets try to make poetry as full and rich as possible in order to secure the maximum of truth and of poetical effect. An experience must be presented in its complexity, without the simplifications and the order which analytical thought gives. Since the originating creative condition is extremely direct and immediate, and often very unfamiliar, the poet must not be afraid to state exactly what he feels and to trust that he will be understood.

C. H. BOWRA: *The Creative Experiment*, 1949

The lyric poem . . . must be 'simple'. This does not necessarily mean 'un-complex' or 'easy to understand'—some lyric poetry is highly complex and difficult. It means that the poem should convey a single mood, a single state of mind, and convey it in a form free from all irrelevancies—a form which seems to have no 'joins' or patches, but fits the mood like a seamless coat.

C. DAY LEWIS: *Poetry for You*, 1944

✤ OBSCURITY ✤

*What we take for bad lighting may be a
dirty windscreen.*

This is a charge which any poet, whose imagination is warm and rapid,
must expect from his contemporaries. Milton did not escape it. . . . If
any man expect from my poetry the same easiness of style which he
admires in a drinking song, for him I have not written.

S. T. COLERIDGE

It is a sentiment that very universally prevails, that poetry is a light
kind of reading, which one takes up only for a little amusement, and
that therefore it should be so perspicuous as not to require a second
reading.

DR J. GREGORY in a letter to Dr Beattie, 1766

Some people with a working vocabulary of, say, 200 words, expect to
be able to take up a poem and read it while toying with breakfast, and
then complain that the poet is not intelligible.

C. L. BOLTZ: *Crown to Mend,* 1945

Genius is the introduction of a new element into the intellectual
universe: or, if that be not allowed, it is the application of powers to
objects on which they had not before been exercised, or the employ-
ment of them in such a manner as to produce effects hitherto unknown.
What is all this but an advance, or a conquest made by the soul of the
poet? Is it to be supposed that the reader can make progress of this
kind, like an Indian prince or general—stretched on his palanquin, and
borne by his slaves? No; he is invigorated and inspirited by his leader,
in order that he may exert himself; for he cannot proceed in quiescence;
he cannot be carried like a dead weight.

WILLIAM WORDSWORTH: Supplementary Essay to *Poems,* 1815

In my opinion that which, being with a little endeavour searched, adds a kind of majesty to Poesy, is better than that which every cobbler may sing to his patch. Obscurity in affection of words and indigested conceits is pedantical and childish; but where it shroudeth itself in the heart of his subject, uttered with fitness of figure and expressive epithets, with that darkness will I still labour to be shadowed. . . .

GEORGE CHAPMAN: Prefatory letter to
Ovid's *Banquet of Sense*, 1595

Remember, also, that the medium through which, in poetry, the heart is to be affected, is language; a thing subject to endless fluctuations and arbitrary associations. The genius of the poet melts these down for his purpose: but they retain their shape and quality to him who is not capable of exerting, within his own mind, a corresponding energy.

WILLIAM WORDSWORTH: Supplementary Essay to *Poems*, 1815

Your lines are not to be understood reading on one leg. . . . Your obscurity, where you are dark, which is seldom, is that of too much meaning, not the painful obscurity which no toil of the reader can dissipate; not the dead vacuum and floundering place in which imagination finds no footing; it is not the dimness of positive darkness, but of distance; and he that reads and not discerns must get a better pair of spectacles.

CHARLES LAMB to Charles Lloyd, Autumn 1823

The difficulty of poetry (and modern poetry is supposed to be difficult) may be due to one of several reasons. First, there may be personal causes which make it impossible for a poet to express himself in any but an obscure way; while this may be regrettable, we should be glad, I think, that the man has been able to express himself at all. Or difficulty may be due just to novelty: we know the ridicule accorded in turn to Wordsworth, Shelley and Keats, Tennyson and Browning. . . . Or difficulty may be caused by the reader's having been told, or having suggested to himself, that the poem is going to prove difficult. The ordinary reader, when warned against the obscurity of a poem, is apt to be thrown into a state of consternation very unfavourable to poetic receptivity. Instead of beginning, as he should, in a state of sensitivity, he obfuscates his senses by the desire to be clever and to look very hard for something, he doesn't know what—or else by the desire not to be taken in. There is such a thing as stage fright, but what such readers have is pit or gallery fright. The more seasoned reader, he who has reached, in these matters, a state of greater *purity*, does not bother about understanding; not, at least, at first. I know that some of the poetry to which I am most devoted is poetry which I did not understand at first reading; some is poetry which I am not sure I understand yet: for instance, Shakespeare's. And finally, there is the difficulty caused by the author's having left out something which the reader is used to finding: so that the reader, bewildered, gropes about for what is absent, and puzzles his head for a kind of 'meaning' which is not there, and is not meant to be there.

T. S. ELIOT: Conclusion to *The Use of Poetry*, 1933

I believe Shakespeare was not a whit more intelligible in his own day than he is now to an educated man, except for a few local allusions of no consequence.

S. T. COLERIDGE: *Table Talk*, 15 March 1834

That magic spirit in Shakespeare's mind that enables—or coerces—him to see one idea from two or three angles simultaneously.

RICHARD FLATTER: *Hamlet's Father*, 1949

That even Shakespeare, or rather, that Shakespeare in particular, is an obscure poet, is witnessed by the numerous volumes of elucidatory criticism which have been devoted to his text. It is a regrettable fact that misprints were not unknown in Shakespeare's time—regrettable because every editor who was not also a poet (and few of them have had even a trace of poetic sensibility) has acted on the presumption that anything he could not understand was due to a printer's error. And so we get the gigantic farce of Shakespearian criticism—the greatest of all monuments to the obliquity of pedants.

> Light thickens, and the Crow
> Makes Wing to the Rookie Wood.

They seize on such absolute poetry as this, and instead of allowing it to work its wonderful magic unchecked, they halt at the word *Rookie*. It doesn't quite make sense. It is redundant. Why should a crow fly to a wood full of rooks? They smell a misprint. Perhaps Shakespeare wrote reeky. German: *Rauch*. Cf. *Auld Reekie* (Scots). That is merely the beginning of the process, for no two textual critics can agree.

Meanwhile the poetry of the passage, which they can never have felt, is forgotten, and Shakespeare becomes the bane of schoolboys.

> HERBERT READ: 'Obscurity in Poetry',
> *Collected Essays in Literary Criticism*, 1938

Before people complain of the obscurity of modern poetry, they should first examine their consciences, and ask themselves with how many people and on how many occasions they have genuinely and profoundly shared some experience with another. . . .

> W. H. AUDEN: 'On Writing Poetry Today', B.B.C., June 1955

◉   ◉   ◉

Despite this defence, one fact remains: justifiable obscurity must be the result of what Lamb called 'too much meaning', or else the state of mind to be communicated is such a complex one that the complexity itself must be conveyed. The unforgivable obscurity derives from a feeling of conscious superiority—'I am Sir Oracle, and when I ope my mouth let no dog bark'—or from a desire to be thought profound by imitating the externals of profundity in better poets.

◉   ◉   ◉

We have to be careful . . . in discriminating between the pretentious wilfulness of the charlatan—the pseudo-poet, often the meretricious imitator of true originality—and what I should like to call, if it isn't too contradictory a phrase, *sincere* obscurity. I mean the case of the poet who is truly struggling to express a difficult thought or elusive experience—perhaps some partly-glimpsed apprehension of a truth— and finding that his present poetic equipment isn't equal to the task.

> MARGARET WILLY: 'The Nature of Poetry',
> address to the English Association, 1956

We cannot be too critical in our examination of what is called obscurity in poetry—in our discrimination between a difficulty in reading the meaning which may be due to profundity or mysticism in the conception, and that which is due to bad workmanship. The obscurity which has no excuse can be traced to four sources:

> The fumblings of a confused mind among its own sensations.
> Ignorance of the value of the language used, and of its syntax and prosody.

Deliberate distortion of that language, with the object of producing an original effect, or of giving an impression of profundity to commonplace thoughts.

The introduction of abstruse allusions, or remote historical references, which convey no meaning to those who are not specialists in certain subjects.

S. R. LYSAGHT: *A Reading of Poetry*, 1934

Some writers appear to believe that emotions gain in intensity through being inarticulate. Perhaps the emotions are not significant enough to endure full daylight.

T. S. ELIOT: 'Rhetoric and Poetic Drama',
The Sacred Wood, 1920

There is also the obscurity which is the result of the poet's wishing to appear mad, even if only a little mad. This is rather common and rather dreadful. I know nothing more distasteful than the work of a poet who has taken leave of his reason deliberately, as a commutor might of his wife.

E. B. WHITE: *One Man's Meat*, 1943

For every clear-headed poet . . . there are at least three hundred of crossword-conscious professors demanding . . . to be *puzzled* by poetry which is more difficult to read than to write; poetry in which they can joyfully hunt the thimble of meaning through haystacks of self-bamboozlement; poetry which is vague and formless but offers (like Leonardo's mildewed wall) a million suggestions of half-meanings and glimmerings of sense.

ROY CAMPBELL in the *Poetry Review*

One of two kinds of clearness one should have—either the meaning to be felt without effort as fast as one reads; or else, if dark at first reading, when once made out, *to explode*.

GERARD MANLEY HOPKINS: *Letters*

✺ ORIGINALITY ✺

Every poet has his own net, and his own draught
of fishes.
ROBERT LYND, 'Poetry and the Modern Man'

The poet must see things with his own eyes, hear them with his own ears; not with the eyes and ears of those who have written before him.

W. H. DAVIES

Poets of low vitality ensconce themselves like hermit-crabs, generation after generation, in the cast-off shells of their predecessors.

JOHN LIVINGSTON LOWES: *Convention and Revolt in Poetry*, 1919

So the originality of a poet lies first and last in the audacity of being which permits him to be true to what he perceives, and to his own nature. There is no true originality apart from this, though some poetry may seem more startlingly original because the reader is unfamiliar with it.

STEPHEN SPENDER: *Life and the Poet*, 1942

There is no new poetry: but the new poet . . . comes with a new note. And that new note it is that troubles the critical waters.

THOMAS HARDY: Notebooks

The revolutionists in poetry are quite the mildest-mannered men that ever scuttled ship or cut a throat.

JOHN LIVINGSTON LOWES

If there be one conclusion more forcibly pressed upon us than another by the review which has been given of the fortunes and fate of poetical Works, it is this—that every author, as far as he is great and at the same time *original*, has had the task of *creating* the taste by which he is to be enjoyed.

WILLIAM WORDSWORTH: Supplementary Essay to *Poems*, 1815

Every powerful personality imposes himself inevitably upon a recipient group of followers. But what he cannot give or they receive is the quality that makes him what he is. That is incommunicable. What he can and does transmit are the accidents, the idiosyncrasies, the mannerisms of his genius. . . . The slopes of Parnassus are crowded with poets clad in the cast-off accidents of genius.

JOHN LIVINGSTON LOWES: *Convention and Revolt in Poetry*, 1919

Modern poetry is characterized by the poet's *anxiety* to be always striking. There is the same march in the Greek and Latin poets. Claudian, who had powers to have been anything—observe in him this anxious, craving vanity! Every line, nay, every word, stops, looks full in your face, and asks and *begs* for praise. . . .

S. T. COLERIDGE: *Anima Poetæ*, 1805

Many of the images of modern poetry are merely astonishing. They lack that definite and *perpetual* surprise-value of the best poetry of all ages.

E. W. F. TOMLIN: Lectures on Modern Poetry, 1936

The way of life which the machine imposes on us, replacing the rhythmical recurrences of Nature by mathematically identical 'soulless' repetitions, has developed in us a horror of all recurrence and a corresponding obsession with novelty. The resistance of most people to poetry, the lack of interest displayed by many contemporary poets in the art of 'numbers', is due, I believe, to their association of repeated pattern with all that is boring and disagreeable in their lives. Similarly, while novelty is good—even the most traditional cultures have demanded that a work of art be in some sense 'original' and not a mere copy—the idolatry of novelty is more destructive than any traditional idolatry and harder to cure. Tristan may be led to see that there is something excessive about his love for Isolde by being reminded that she will die; Don Giovanni cannot be cured in this way, because you cannot tell him that the supply of ladies will run out.

W. H. AUDEN in a foreword to *An Armada of Thirty Whales*,
by Daniel G. Hoffman

In Poetry I have a few Axioms, and you will see how far I am from their Centre. First, I think Poetry should surprise by a fine excess and not by Singularity—it should strike the Reader as a wording of his own highest thoughts, and appear almost a Remembrance.

JOHN KEATS in a letter to John Taylor, 27 February 1818

Poetry should be great and unobtrusive, a thing which enters into one's soul and does not startle it or amaze it with itself, but with its subject.

JOHN KEATS in a letter to John Hamilton Reynolds,
3 February 1818

Those only who feel no originality, no consciousness of having received their thoughts and opinions from immediate inspiration, are anxious to be thought original.

S. T. COLERIDGE: *Anima Poetæ*, 1805

The current notion that *invention* is a mark of high originality is one of the vulgar errors that dies hard. If it were true, 'The House of a Thousand Candles' or the 'Filigree Ball' would bear away the palm from many a masterpiece. But it is not the case. None of the great poets has ever troubled himself particularly to invent. . . .

Originality, then, is independent of invention. It is rather the gift of seeing and seizing the latent possibilities of familiar things. We accept that formulation without demur when the familiar things are the appearances of earth, and air, and sea, and sky—effects of light and shade, nuances of colour, aspects of mass and line, sound, fragrance, movement—all the bewildering, irridescent throng of old impressions that all at once flash into new, when the eye is quickened and alert. What we fail, perhaps, to realize is this: that the old and well-worn forms of art, the familiar treatments of traditional themes, stand to the poet in precisely the same relation as the world of eye and ear. And they too may flash into life under the same compelling vision that at rare moments pierces the husk of *things*, and discloses beauty.

JOHN LIVINGSTON LOWES: *Convention and Revolt in Poetry*, 1919

One error, in fact, of eccentricity in poetry is to seek for new human emotions to express; and in this search for novelty in the wrong place it discovers the perverse.

T. S. ELIOT: 'Tradition and Individual Talent'

True originality is merely development; and if it is right development it may appear in the end so *inevitable* that we almost come to the point of view of denying all 'original' virtue to the poet. He simply did the next thing.

T. S. ELIOT: Introduction to Ezra Pound's *Selected Poems*, 1928

❧ TRADITION ❧

Cut the connection with the great reservoir of past achieve-
ment, and the stream runs shallow, and the substance of
poetry becomes tenuous and thin.
JOHN LIVINGSTON LOWES

People are always talking about originality; but what do they mean?
As soon as we are born, the world begins to work upon us, and this
goes on to the end. What can we call our own except energy, strength,
and will? If I could give an account of all that I owe to great predecessors and contemporaries, there would be but a small balance in
my favour.
J. W. GOETHE to Eckermann, 12 May 1825

No poet, no artist of any art, has his complete meaning alone. His
significance, his appreciation is the appreciation of his relation to the
dead poets and artists. You cannot value him alone; you must set
him, for contrast and comparison, among the dead.
T. S. ELIOT

A poem read in its final form may seem miraculous. But it becomes less
of a miracle and more of a piece of fine craftsmanship when we think of
it in relation to the generations of writers who have gone before,
slowly forging the tool which the man we admire can wield with such
apparent ease.
DESMOND FLOWER: Foreword to *The Pursuit of Poetry*, 1939

Tradition . . . is a sort of compost, to whose making has gone the
poetry of many centuries and countries.
C. DAY LEWIS

Happy is the poet who has the heritage of a great language to work
with, even as the architect is fortunate who has stone quarries and
not brickfields at his command.

S. R. LYSAGHT: *A Reading of Poetry*, 1934

The vitality of tradition and the quickening impulse of immediate contact with reality—it is the fructifying influence of each of these upon the other that makes for life in poetry. Either without the other means sterility.

                                        JOHN LIVINGSTON LOWES

Poetry, like the other arts—like the human race itself—needs both tradition and experiment to keep it alive.

                                                    C. DAY LEWIS

The critic requires a detachment from the prepossessions of his own time; as he returns to a poem, he surrenders himself wholly to it. He has for his goal that particular completion which the impulse of the writer found in the poem itself, and, going from impulse to poem, his understanding will now be more intimate. The poet, on the other hand, bringing with him his own creative tendency, the direction of which owes a great deal to the current of ideas active in his own time, takes up what he can of the still flowing impulses, to carry them on to a new and unforeseeable creation. No longer under the tyranny of the poems, he is inspired by the succession of the poets.

        G. ROSTREVOR HAMILTON: 'The Meaning of Tradition',
                                    The Tell-Tale Article, 1949

In poetry, as in the State, it is after all a constitutional régime, tempered by occasional revolution, that remains the least objectionable mode that has been found of muddling through.

                                        JOHN LIVINGSTON LOWES

It is part of the business of the critic to preserve tradition—where a good tradition exists. It is part of his business to see literature steadily and to see it whole; and this is eminently to see it not as consecrated by time, but to see it beyond time; to see the best work of our time and the best work of twenty-five hundred years ago with the same eyes.

        T. S. ELIOT: Introduction to The Sacred Wood, 1920

No doubt, when we get beyond externals to the universe of the poem itself, a certain similarity does exist between the modern poet and the seventeenth-century metaphysical, but that similarity cannot be

L

resolved chemically into identity plus difference. When the modern poet is original, he is so by reason of his whole being, and not by reason of separate and distinct elements in his make-up. He is original because he is traditional: that is to say, because ways of thought and feeling which were active in such and such poets of the past have endured in the only way that things of the mind can endure, by being permeated through and through with change. We have here the paradox of all vital experience, cracking the inadequate moulds of our ordinary thought and available language. The stream is the same, yet not the same: *change, no less than permanence, is the essence of tradition, internal to it, and not added from outside.*

G. ROSTREVOR HAMILTON:'The Meaning of Tradition',
The Tell-Tale Article, 1949

The task of the poet is to connect the remotest past with the furthest future.

R. M. RILKE

❦ TODAY ❦

*The poet must be tuned to receive the meanings of his own
time. He must also be earthed in tradition.*

C. DAY LEWIS

If the poetry and the intelligence of the age lose touch with each other,
poetry will cease to matter much, and the age will be lacking in finer
awareness.

F. R. LEAVIS: *New Bearings in English Poetry*, 1932

It has to be living, to learn the speech of the place,
It has to face the man of the time.

WALLACE STEVENS: 'Of Modern Poetry'

A poet should express the emotion of all the ages and the thought of
his own.

THOMAS HARDY: Notebooks

Poets who leave their own time out of their work cannot be surprised
if their time fails to find them interesting. The life and thought about
us must be the foundation of our life and thought. Those poets who
shrink from the life about them, however skilfully they may invent or
imagine, will appeal, in the main, not to the world but to those few
who, like themselves, cannot or will not face the world.

JOHN MASEFIELD: *With the Living Voice*, 1925

The best poetry is always of its age as well as for all time; a poet is
nourished by the soil, and conditioned by the climate, in which he has
grown up. A knowledge of these influences helps towards a fuller
appreciation of every sort of poetry, but it is especially valuable when
we are dealing with the kind called 'philosophical'. Some poets may
be seers, but they can only see what is visible from where they stand.

BASIL WILLEY: Broadcast talk, 'Poetry and Philosophy',

The Listener, 2 February 1950

The great poet, in writing himself, writes his time.

T. S. ELIOT

The poet is a prophet only in so far as he has an audience in his own time. To wait for the future with which he is already abreast is to deliver his message too late. The poet should point out what is happening *while* it is happening: he is not there to deliver funeral orations. This, if it is true, places a terrible burden of responsibility on the poet. His antennae must be moving, his feelers waving with a feverish intensity.

J. ISAACS: The Background to Modern Poetry, 1951

Poetry is the purest medium through which the contemporary sensibility makes itself known.

E. W. F. TOMLIN

Good poetry of any age is good forever: the point is that in order to *be* good poetry, it must be the expression of actual and immediate experience at first hand, the vision of the eternal through what *is*, here and now—not through what *was*, yesterday. . . . Somehow or other, poetry has always to come to terms with the modern contemporary consciousness.

AUBREY DE SELINCOURT: On Reading Poetry, 1952

A poet cannot choose his time or his subject-matter, any more than we can choose the parents who give birth to us. But in accepting the limitations of his time, and using them as the harness of his genius, the great poet transcends it.

C. DAY LEWIS: The Poet's Task, 1951

❧ RECOGNITION ❧

I felt a wind upon my face from heaven.—
W. SCAWEN BLUNT

The finest poetry gives a shock of instant recognition, like a revenant from one's own past. Perhaps that is why the physical sensation it produces is so reminiscent of ghost-stories—the porcupine hair and cooling spine.

❋   ❋   ❋

I know no theory of poetical truth more satisfactory than what I have heard called the 'Click Theory'. If it has connections with the spinal shiver theory, that is not my fault nor a fault of the theory. The spinal shiver which follows something consummately said, all save the coolest natures know well. It is the comment of the emotions when the hand of the master is laid upon them. The 'Click Theory' goes a little further. Something is said, and all the intricate words at once of the infinitely mysterious mechanism of a human nature, turn; all the parts of us meet decisively, yet softly, falling into place with that swift noiseless *click* which is the unresisting assent of the totality of what we are.

H. W. GARROD: 'Poets and Philosophers',
The Profession of Poetry, 1929

A year or two ago, in common with others, I received from America a request that I would define poetry. I replied that I could no more define poetry than a terrier can define a rat, but that I thought we both recognized the object by the symptoms which it provokes in us. One of these symptoms was described by Eliphaz the Temanite: 'A spirit passed before my face: the hair of my flesh stood up.'

Experience has taught me, when I am shaving of a morning, to keep watch over my thoughts, because, if a line of poetry strays into my memory, my skin bristles so that the razor ceases to act. This particular sensation is accompanied by a shiver down the spine; there is another which consists in a constriction of the throat and a precipitation of water to the eyes; and there is a third which I can only describe by borrowing a phrase from one of Keats's last letters where he says, speaking of Fanny Brawne: 'Everything that reminds me of her goes through me like a spear.' The seat of this sensation is the pit of the stomach.

A. E. HOUSMAN: *The Name and Nature of Poetry*, 1933

If I read a book and it makes my whole body so cold no fire can ever warm me, I know that is poetry. If I feel physically as if the top of my head were taken off, I know that is poetry. These are the only ways I know it. Is there any other way?

EMILY DICKINSON in a letter to Thomas Wentworth Higginson

Some poems give me that quickened sense of pleasure somewhere in the back of my head—at the top of my spine I believe it is.

STEPHEN HAGGARD to Christopher Hassall in a letter
quoted in *The Timeless Quest*, 1948

This [a passage from *In Memoriam*] is great poetry, economical of words, a universal emotion related to a particular place; and it gives me the shudder that I fail to get from anything in *Maud*.

T. S. ELIOT: Introduction to the poems of Tennyson, 1936

⁂

My own preference is for goose-flesh. Poetry can sometimes keep the skin on my face tingling for minutes at a time. Always with the greatest work there is this physical recognition, accompanying or even preceding mental understanding. And when poetry has such an effect as this, it is no use the critics rushing up to tell us what points to admire: the poet has got there first.

⁂

The experience of a poem is the experience both of a moment and of a lifetime. It is very much like our intenser experiences of other human beings. There is a first, or an early moment which is unique, of shock and surprise, even of terror . . . a moment which can never be forgotten, but which is never repeated integrally; and yet which would become destitute of significance if it did not survive in a larger whole of experience: which survives inside a deeper and a calmer feeling.

T. S. ELIOT: *Dante*, 1929

❧ THE READER ❧

Poetry, good or bad, depends for its very life on the hospitable reader, as tinder awaits the spark.
WALTER DE LA MARE, 'The Green Room'

To have great poets there must be great audiences too.

WALT WHITMAN

The simple way to arrive at an appreciation of poetry is to read it—and then to read it again.

DESMOND FLOWER: *The Pursuit of Poetry*, 1939

One gets the impression from so many readers of poetry that they are embarrassed, almost as though they had been asked to discuss their love affairs at a public meeting. But reading poetry is as natural an activity as eating one's breakfast.

VICARS BELL: *On Learning the English Tongue*, 1953

Poetry is like shot-silk with many glancing colours. Every reader must find his own interpretation according to his ability, and according to his sympathy with the poet.

ALFRED TENNYSON, quoted in Hallam Tennyson's *Memoirs*

The impression a poem gives seems to me like a child begotten by the poet's thoughts on the reader's, in 'a marriage of true minds'.

F. L. LUCAS: *Decline and Fall of the Romantic Ideal*, 1936

Without aiming here at accuracy, we may say that an actual poem is the succession of experiences—sounds, images, thoughts, emotions—through which we pass when we are reading as poetically as we can.

A. G. BRADLEY: *Oxford Lectures on Poetry*, 1909

Sympathetic understanding means . . . imaginative effort—your true reader of poetry is always a bit of a poet himself.

JOHN LIVINGSTON LOWES

The process of getting to understand a poet is precisely that of constructing his poem in one's own mind.

WILLIAM EMPSON: *Seven Types of Ambiguity*, 1930

*   *   *

But this reconstruction has to be to the poet's specifications. We must not give too important a place to the scaffolding called 'intellectual content':

. . . the agitation which is the experience [of reading poetry] divides into a major and a minor branch, though the two streams have innumerable interconnections and influence one another intimately. Indeed, it is only as an expositor's artifice that we may speak of them as two streams.

The minor branch we may call the intellectual stream: the other, which we may call the active, or emotional stream, is made up of the play of our interests. The intellectual stream is comparatively easy to follow; it follows itself, so to speak; but it is the less important of the two. In poetry it matters only *as a means*; it directs and excites the active stream. It is made up of thoughts, which are not static little entities that bob up into consciousness and down again out of it, but fluent happenings, events, which refer or point to the things the thoughts are 'of' . . .

Some people who read verse (they do not often read much of it) are so constituted that very little more happens than this intellectual stream of thoughts. It is perhaps superfluous to point out that they miss the real poem. To exaggerate this part of the experience, and give it too much importance on its own account, is a notable current tendency and for many people explains why they do not read poetry. The active branch is what really matters: for from it all the energy of the whole agitation comes. The thinking which goes on is somewhat like the play of an ingenious and invaluable 'governor' run by but controlling the main machine.

I. A. RICHARDS: *Science and Poetry*, 1935

The first step in appreciating poetry is to learn the three R's—Rhythm, Rhyme, Repetition—for all poetry is based upon them. They are the instruments which communicate the magic of poetry; the movements and intonations of the hypnotist. For poetry is, among other things, a kind of hypnosis; it puts one part of us asleep in order that another part may become more aware, more receptive, more active. If we pit our will against the hypnotist, he is powerless; if we resist the influence of a poem, it will fail in its main purpose, which is to speak direct to our heart.

C. DAY LEWIS: *Enjoying Poetry*, 1947

Only genuine poetry will give to the reader who approaches it in the proper manner a response which is as passionate, noble and serene as the experience of the poet, the master of speech, because in the creative moment he is the master of experience itself.

I. A. RICHARDS: *Science and Poetry*, 1935

On the other hand, there is the danger of too emotional a response— of identifying our feelings too exclusively with the poet's, or, more dangerous still, compelling his feelings to identify themselves with ours:

[A quite uninitiated reader] is unable to distinguish the poetry from an emotional state aroused in himself by the poetry, a state which may be merely an indulgence of his own emotions. The poetry may be an accidental stimulus. The end of the enjoyment of poetry is a pure contemplation from which all the accidents of personal emotion are removed.

T. S. ELIOT: 'The Perfect Critic', *The Sacred Wood*, 1920

. . . the reading of poetry is not a species of poetic abandon, not an unreined emotional excitation, but is an ordering and controlling of the intellectual and emotional experience to which the poem gives expression.

P. GURREY: *The Appreciation of Poetry*, 1935

The . . . mature stage of enjoyment of poetry comes when we cease to identify ourselves with the poet we happen to be reading; when our critical faculties remain awake; when we are aware of what one poet can be expected to give and what he cannot. The poem has its own existence, apart from us. . . .

T. S. ELIOT: *The Use of Poetry and the Use of Criticism*, 1933

The ideal reader must be sensitive to words over their whole poetic range, and respond to poetry musically, emotionally, imaginatively, and in other ways besides.

KATHARINE M. WILSON: *Sound and Meaning in English Poetry*, 1930

⊛   ⊛   ⊛

The right balance in the reader's mind is when the emotional and intellectual responses are united. This requires either a Garden of Eden innocence—one recalls T. S. Eliot's definition of an ideal audience for poetic drama as being one which can neither read nor write—or else a self-consciousness that has regained the imaginative paradise by fighting its way through education and coming out the other side. In either case, the key to the garden is enjoyment.

⊛   ⊛   ⊛

Complete unsophistication and complete sophistication—natural and acquired wisdom—are poetry's friends. It is superficial culture, the iron frost of partial self-consciousness, the treacherous thin ice of elementary knowledge, that render the approaches to poetry impassable for so many.

C. DAY LEWIS: *A Hope for Poetry*, 1936

. . the act of knowing is itself an act of sympathizing; unless you are enjoying the poetry you cannot create it, as poetry, in your mind.

WILLIAM EMPSON: *Seven Types of Ambiguity*,
Revised edition, 1947

Liking poetry is better than lumping it; but it is not the same as loving.

WALTER DE LA MARE in a broadcast talk

❧ THE CRITIC: CONS ❧

It is difficult . . . to become a
critic and remain a man.
WILLIAM ALLINGHAM

People who would think it impertinent to question the findings of the
Astronomer Royal . . . and who would listen with respectful silence to
an expert on gardening, burst into clamour over a book of poems or a
piece of sculpture, though their knowledge of these things may be no
greater than their knowledge of astronomy or horticulture.

NORMAN CALLAN: *Poetry in Practice,* 1938

Our critics are often interested in extracting something from their
subject which is not fairly in it.
T. S. ELIOT

. . . that tendency in so much modern scholarship in which the estab-
ment of a new jargon for restating old ideas is looked upon as an
increase in perception.
JOHN CIARDI: *New York Times*

Criticism of poetry moves between two extremes. On the one hand
the critic may busy himself so much with the implications of a poem
or of one poet's work—implications moral, social, religious, or other—
that the poetry becomes hardly more than a text for a discourse. . . .
Or if you stick too closely to the 'poetry', and adopt no attitude
towards what the poet has to say, you will tend to evacuate it of all
significance.
T. S. ELIOT: 'Age of Dryden',
The Use of Poetry, 1933

I know nothing that surpasses the vileness of deciding on the merits of
a poet . . . by accidental failures or faulty passages.

S. T. COLERIDGE: *Biographia Literaria,* 1817

The crying sin of modern criticism is that it is overloaded with personality. If an author commit an error, there is no wish to set him right for the sake of truth, but for the sake of triumph. . . .

S. T. COLERIDGE: First Lecture on Shakespeare, 1811–12

I cannot feel happy about that school of modern criticism which treats literature as a mine-field, to be approached in a suspicious attitude, with infinite caution and detectors held out in front of one; nor do I believe the chief task of the critic to be the exploding of reputations, however scientific the instruments employed, however reassuring may seem the fashionable code-word for the process.

C. DAY LEWIS: *The Poet's Task*, 1951

Critics . . . are of two sorts: those who merely relieve themselves against the flower of beauty, and those, less continent, who afterwards scratch it up. I myself, I must confess, aspire to the second of these classes; unexplained beauty arouses an irritation in me, a sense that this would be a good place to scratch; the reasons that make a line of verse likely to give pleasure, I believe, are like the reasons for anything else; one can reason about them; and while it may be true that the roots of beauty ought not to be violated, it seems to me very arrogant of the appreciative critic to think that he could do this, if he chose, by a little scratching.[1]

WILLIAM EMPSON: *Seven Types of Ambiguity*,
Revised edition, 1947

Beauty is not limited to what can be seen or heard or measured or poked. . . . Neither for poetry nor for criticism is cleverness enough.

F. L. LUCAS: *The Decline and Fall of the Romantic Ideal*, 1936

To [a certain type of critic] words are merely like algebraic symbols; his mind concentrates on the barest literal meaning; to let it wander away to half-conscious associations would be reprehensible woolgathering. He did not guess that such wool might be the Golden Fleece of poetry.

F. L. LUCAS: *The same*

---

[1] Few critics, unfortunately, are sufficiently garden-trained to replant a flower after scratching it up.

... the worth cannot be abstracted from the poem like the wavelength of a light from its colour, and given a measure. It must be judged, as it must be made, by the whole soul of man. That is why great criticism, like great poetry, has not been written by little men.

J. BRONOWSKI: *The Poet's Defence*, 1939

If you parse a poem and break it up into its separate parts of speech, you may find out a good deal about its construction, and how this resembles the construction of other poems. But as long as you fix your attention only on the grammar you must miss all that is really important about the poem. The same is true of all analysis. If you were to be handed over to the chemist for him to work on, he would analyse your body into its chemical constituents and could find out exactly what substances it was made of. He might even present your executors with a row of little bottles, all neatly labelled, containing the separate substances of which you were made. But still there would remain a good deal about you of which he could say nothing. . . .

JOHN PILLEY, quoted by Walter de la Mare, from
An Outline of Knowledge for Boys and Girls and their Parents

Let us face the day when every leap of the heart that literature gives us shall be duly charted and analysed in coloured inks; but that day is not yet in sight. And I shall not pray for it. Its dawn may well prove a triumph for science rather than for art. The more we discover of what we call the 'unconscious', the more we may doubt the benefit of dragging up into the light of consciousness impulses that for the poets and readers of three thousand years have worked unconsciously. . . . In the Aran Islands, I gather, they believe that to talk too much of the the things of fairy may turn the tongue to stone. It happens. I have seen it.

F. L. LUCAS: *The Decline and Fall of the Romantic Ideal*, 1936

... that barren type of classification so dear to those who believe that if they can invent a few transcendental pigeon-holes, the Holy Spirit of poetry will descend to nest in them.

F. L. LUCAS: *The same*

✣ THE CRITIC : PROS ✣

It is not true that criticism is a luxury trade. The rear-guard of society cannot be extricated until the vanguard has gone further.
I. A. RICHARDS, *Principles of Literary Criticism*

The critic's first duty is neither to condemn nor to praise, but to elucidate technique and meaning.

MICHAEL ROBERTS: *A Critique of Poetry*, 1934

The critic has one pre-eminent task—the task of easing or widening or deepening our response to poetry. There are, of course, many ways of performing this task. But no critical method will satisfactorily perform it, if there is not respect both for the poem and for the reader.

C. DAY LEWIS: *The Poetic Image*, 1947

. . . a literary critic should have no emotions except those immediately provoked by a work of art. . . .

T. S. ELIOT

A critic should often be in a position to say, 'I don't like this but I know it is good', or 'I like this and condemn it . . .'

T. S. ELIOT

If I ask by what means a critic principally achieves his business of being interesting and giving pleasure, there are three virtues which seem to me, beyond all others, to come into question. They are: the range of his information, the variety of his method, and the emphasis of his personality. . . . Poetry means something, and we cannot tolerate that a man should speak of it as though it did not mean something to him.

H. W. GARROD: *Poetry and the Criticism of Life*, 1931

Since nothing could be more confusing than the idea that criticism functions as a sort of separate destructive element whose object is the works of the poet, it would be as well to arrive at a definition of the terms 'critic' and 'criticism', and of one or two others which will have to be employed in describing the critical and the creative activities. I shall use *criticism* to mean a complete judgment or valuation of a poem, and *critic* to mean one who makes such a judgment. But in case it should appear that criticism involves only one kind of activity (loosely called critical) and that this activity is the property of the critic but not of the poet, I would point out that to write a poem, no less than to criticize it, demands just such a judgment as we have in mind, and that therefore a poem is also a criticism. In this respect the activities of creation and criticism are parallel; and it will be seen that the parallel goes even further.

The primary activity of the poet's mind is that of imagination, which may be described as 'the entertainment of new entities'. The poet relates ideas hitherto unrelated, and in so doing makes a synthesis which we call a poem. When the mind of the critic turns to this poem it has to do two things: it has to take to pieces the poet's synthesis (this activity I shall call analysis); then it must build up its own synthesis by entering into the poet's thoughts, realizing what new correlations have been made, and valuing them. This process of entering into the poet's thought I shall call appreciation: it is only possible through the exercise of imagination.

NORMAN CALLAN: *Poetry in Practice*, 1938

❀   ❀   ❀

Does it follow, then, that a poet is likely to prove the best of critics? Opinions differ on this question, even among poets.

❀   ❀   ❀

While there is a great mass of valuable criticism done by critics who were only critics, the most valuable criticism of all, the only quite essential criticism, has been done by creative writers, for the most part poets.

ARTHUR SYMONS: Introduction to
Biographia Literaria (Everyman Edn.)

Byron uttered upon almost all the poets judgments preposterous beyond belief. Scott could be relied upon to think almost any poetry

good. Wordsworth had a way of thinking even the best poetry bad—
if he had not written it himself.

H. W. GARROD: Poetry and the Criticism of Life, 1931

The sentimental person, in whom a work of art arouses all sorts of
emotions which have nothing to do with that work of art whatever,
but are accidents of personal association, is an incomplete artist. For in
an artist these suggestions made by a work of art, which are purely
personal, become fused with a multitude of other suggestions from
multitudinous experience, and result in the production of a new object
which is no longer purely personal, because it is a work of art itself. . . .
This gives us an intimation why the artist is—each within his own
limitations—oftenest to be depended upon as a critic; his criticism will
be criticism, and not the satisfaction of a suppressed creative wish.

T. S. ELIOT: 'The Perfect Critic', The Sacred Wood, 1920

When the critics are themselves poets, it may be suspected that they
have formed their critical statements with a view to justifying their
poetic practice.

T. S. ELIOT: Introduction to the Use of Poetry, 1933

Sir, I am a better judge of mutton than any sheep.

SAMUEL JOHNSON

❋   ❋   ❋

Poets, then, may not be the best judges of other people's work. Are
they even reliable critics of their own?

❋   ❋   ❋

Even as truth is its own light and evidence, discovering at once itself
and falsehood, so is it the prerogative of poetic genius to distinguish by
parental instinct its proper offspring from the changelings, which the
gnomes of vanity or the fairies of fashion may have laid in its cradle or
called by its names.[1]   S. T. COLERIDGE: <i>Biographia Literaria</i>, 1817

❋   ❋   ❋

---

[1] This is not a perfect analogy. Sometimes, in the less inspired poems of Coleridge himself and Wordsworth, one feels that a little gnome-work, a changeling
or two, would have made all the difference.

On the whole, I think, a poet is not likely to be a reliable critic of his own verse, for he is too close to it. He remembers too clearly the circumstances in which it was written—the thing or person or idea that started it moving; the wall or hedge he was passing at the time, the way the sun was slanting through a particular tree. How can he disentangle all these facts from the words to which they are no longer relevant? The poem has an independent life, a personality of its own; but the poet, like the mother, is always aware of some personal connection.

Moreover, self-criticism, though it might have led Wordsworth to smother some of his more fatuous lines at birth, could have prevented the conception of his more celestial ones. Self-criticism, carried too far, becomes self-distrust. The artist begins to question his inspiration, and to interfere with the unconscious depths of poetry which should remain unconscious. Nevertheless, though the poet is an uncertain judge of his own works, he is (in spite of Professor Garrod's examples) the most reliable critic of poetry in general. From Sir Philip Sidney, Shelley and Keats, to T. S. Eliot and Day Lewis in our own time, he is able to bring to criticism some of that creative love which has gone to the making of his own verse. Some other critics, it is true, have regarded poetry in this light—A. C. Bradley and Livingston Lowes in particular—but too often the non-poet sacrifices imagination to cleverness and classification. He throws out the baby and analyses the bath-water.

M

❧ SOUND AND MUSIC ❧

Poetry is a spoken and not a written art.
Imagist Manifesto

Our debt to the printing press is great—so great that it is vain to try to measure it—but it has not all been gain, and one of the losses to the people in general is that they no more hear the voice of poetry.

ALEXANDER HADDOW: *On the Teaching of Poetry*, 1926

It is for the ear, not for the eye, that poetry is written.

JOHN LIVINGSTON LOWES

No poetry which, when mastered, is not better heard than read, is good poetry.

W. H. AUDEN

Poetry is always wanted; it is a need of the human heart. Sincere thought is always wanted. Excitement is always wanted. When either is aimed by a voice and mind right into the human heart, it is irresistible.

JOHN MASEFIELD: *With the Living Voice*, 1925

I am convinced that much of the rather anxious confusion about poetry to be seen in both young students and older readers is caused by an education that has depended too much on silent reading and has cultivated silence as a virtue—too little on any human voice except the didactic voice of the teacher. Unfortunately, trained voices are rare, and untrained voices, especially in the teaching profession, are liable to lose their natural beauty and freshness through strain. Poetry, as much as drama, is meant to be performed, to be heard, rather than read with the eye. . . .

MARJORIE BOULTON: *The Anatomy of Poetry*, 1953

The first things to occur [in a satisfactory reading of poetry]—if they do not, the rest of the experience will be gravely inadequate—are the sound of the words 'in the mind's ear', and the feel of the words imaginarily spoken. These together give the *full body*, as it were, to the words, and it is with the full bodies of words that the poet works, not with their printed signs. The full bodies reflect the whole meaning of the words as the printed signs cannot. But many people lose nearly everything in poetry through failure to develop this indispensable and controlling reflection.

I. A. RICHARDS: *Science and Poetry*, 1935

What I call the 'auditory imagination' is the feeling for syllable and rhythm, penetrating far below the conscious levels of thought and feeling, invigorating every word; sinking to the most primitive and forgotten, returning to the origin and bringing something back, seeking the beginning and the end.

T. S. ELIOT: 'Matthew Arnold', *The Use of Poetry*, 1933

Poetry withers and dries out when it leaves music, or at least imagined music, too far behind it. Poets who are not interested in music are, or become, bad poets.

EZRA POUND, quoted by J. M. Gibbon in
'Melody and the Lyric'

Today music and speech are far enough apart; it may seem that we talk of the 'music of poetry' only as a figure of speech, indicating no more than the pleasant noise of poetry, and not referring to a fact as we talk of mica in granite. Yet even today poetry is really a music, and if we trace speech and music back into the past or into the primitive, we travel along converging lines.

KATHARINE M. WILSON: *Sound and Meaning in English Poetry*, 1930

Did speech develop out of music, or did music come from speech, or did they start together from a pre-music, pre-speech ancestor, and become differentiated only later? Just as we do not find rhythm existing before melody (though we find it apart from melody), or melody before rhythm, and, though we may differentiate them, we cannot say one grew out of the other, so, far back in distant psychology, perhaps speech had no pre-music existence nor music a pre-speech, but both were parts of the same thing.

KATHARINE M. WILSON: *The same*

All art constantly aspires to the condition of music. For while in all other works of art it is possible to distinguish the matter from the form, and the understanding can always make this distinction, yet it is the constant effort of art to obliterate it. . . .

WALTER PATER: *The Renaissance*, 1873

Why should poetry aspire to the condition of music, any more than music aspires to the condition of poetry? . . . Music is not a more ideal art because its medium is simpler. It might equally well be argued that poetry is the ideal art because, being the only one which uses intellectual meaning as part of its medium, it is the richest. . . .

DAVID DAICHES: *The Place of Meaning in Poetry*, 1935

If poetry is merely music, then what a thin and monotone music it is in comparison with real music! If Baudelaire is only music, what a poverty-stricken music he is in comparison with, say, Wagner. . . . The truth is that, though there can be no poetry without a certain verbal music, yet it is so special a kind of music that it would probably be better to find some other name for it.

H. W. GARROD: *The Profession of Poetry*, 1929

No effects produced by sound are legitimate in poetry which fail in any degree to represent thought.

G. L. RAYMOND: *Poetry as a Representative Art*, 1899

The meaning which forms itself deep in the womb of poetic intuition must find its melody; must, in a sense, *be* its melody, so that the two are quite inseparable. Thus the melody must be there from the beginning, inevitable and innate.

Reviewer in *The Times Literary Supplement* on
Creative Intuition in Art and Poetry

The music of poetry is not something which exists apart from meaning. Otherwise, we could have poetry of great musical beauty which made no sense, and I have never come across such poetry.

T. S. ELIOT: *The Music of Poetry*, 1942

... the walloping dactyllic metre [of Poe's 'City by the Sea'] is all too musical. Poetry ought to be musical, but musical with tact, subtly and variously.

ALDOUS HUXLEY: *Vulgarity in Literature*, 1940

There was a period of the cult of Pure Sound when infants were read passages from Homer, and then questioned as to their impressions—not unlike Darwin playing the trombone to his French beans.

WILLIAM EMPSON: *Seven Types of Ambiguity*, 1947

The supreme poets do not attend to the sound of their poems to make their poetry merely more pleasant or acceptable, but use it just as they make use of all the other resources of words: in order to express what otherwise would be inexpressible.

P. GURREY: *The Appreciation of Poetry*, 1935

There are no gloomy and no sad vowels or syllables, and the army of critics who have attempted to analyse the effects of passages into vowel and consonantal collocations have, in fact, been merely amusing themselves. The way in which the sound of a word is taken varies with the emotion already in being. . . . We should not attribute to the sound alone virtues which involve so many other factors. To say this is not in the least to belittle the importance of the sound; in most cases it is the key to the effects of poetry.

I. A. RICHARDS: *Principles of Literary Criticism*, 1924

◉   ◉   ◉

It is surprising what nonsense is written, by otherwise intelligent people, on the sounds of poetry. Quiller-Couch, after quoting

> And am no more worthy to be called thy son,

instructed us to 'Mark the deep O's' and underlined them for our benefit. In point of fact, each of these five O's is a completely different sound. Only the accident of spelling, where an alphabet of 26 letters is expected to do the work of 45 spoken vowels and conconants, is responsible for their being represented by the same letter. It is even worse when this ignorance of elementary phonetics is allied to the kind of pseudo-mystical portentousness that one associates with handbooks on palmistry and numerology.

This is not to say that the music of poetry is unimportant. It is of supreme importance; and the greater the poem, the more the sound and the sense are one. But as T. S. Eliot has said, 'The music of poetry is the music latent in the common speech of its time.' It is useless attempting to analyse the sounds of verse without having at least a rudimentary knowledge of the sounds of speech. Ultimately the music of poetry is the music of the human voice.

❧ COMMON SPEECH ❧

A man's most vivid emotional and sensuous experience is
inevitably bound up with the language he actually speaks.
F. R. LEAVIS, *New Bearings in English Poetry*

By keeping close to human speech our poetry keeps close to the human heart.

Leader in *The Times Literary Supplement*

The very greatest effects of poetry are often produced without the use of a single word which might not be employed in ordinary speech.

JOHN LIVINGSTON LOWES

The poetry of a people takes its life from the people's speech, and in turn gives life to it.

T. S. ELIOT

At no time, I know, are the written and the spoken language identical. Obviously they cannot be: if we talked extempore as we write, no one would listen; and if we wrote exactly as we talk, no one would read. But speech can never divorce itself beyond some point from the written word without damage to itself; and writing can never beyond some point alienate itself from speech without self-destruction.

T. S. ELIOT: Broadcast talk on John Dryden

Almost anyone is *capable* of a vivid use of language without even noticing it, not only in the metaphors and similes they have accepted on trust from their parents and grandparents, but in expressions of their own coining. . . . During the war there was a report in the papers of two miners who went poaching. They were leaving a wood in darkness when John decided to unload, and accidentally the gun was discharged. This is how John told the story at the inquest on Arthur. 'I looked at Arthur and saw that he stood withering on his feet. I said,

"Have I shot thee?" He said, "Aye." I said, "Is thee bad?" He said, "Aye." I said, "Are thee going to dee?" He said "Aye".'

What poet could do better than 'he stood withering on his feet?' Or, indeed, than the rest of it? This is where poetry and common speech need no adjustment to become one.

CHRISTOPHER FRY: 'Return of a Prodigal', Vogue, U.S.A.

I have known an old fish-wife, who had lost two sons at sea, clench her first at the advancing tide on a stormy day, and cry out: 'Ay! roar, do! How I hates to see thee show thy white teeth.' Now if I had adopted her exclamation and put it into the mouth of some old woman in one of my poems, I dare say the critics would have thought it original enough, but would most likely have advised me to go to Nature for my old woman and not to my own imagination.

ALFRED TENNYSON in a letter to George Dawson,
21 November 1882

The writer of prose, whose material is prosaic, need never diverge very far from the spoken language; and it has been well pointed out that the habit of good conversation probably had something to do with the growth of that lucid and simple prose-style which was the crowning glory of the eighteenth century. But since poets, unlike prose writers, learn more from other poets, and are conservative when they are not great, they are apt to lose touch with the language spoken by their fellow-men.

OWEN BARFIELD: Poetic Diction, 1928

. . . the important changes in the idiom of English verse which are represented by the names of Dryden and Wordsworth, may be characterized as successful attempts to escape from a poetic idiom which had ceased to have a relation to contemporary speech.

T. S. ELIOT: 'Milton', 1947

He must, like the sculptor, be faithful to the medium in which he works; it is out of sounds that he has heard that he must make his melody and harmony.

T. S. ELIOT: The Music of Poetry, 1942

From Chaucer to Thomas Hardy, there has scarcely been a single great English poet of whom we cannot surmise that his style was to some degree influenced by the common speech he heard in field or street: Spenser and Milton are the only possible exceptions. Nevertheless, if we turn from the great individual poets to the successive types and schools of poetry, we do find a periodic, though not a regular, swing of the pendulum between two extremes: between a highly wrought, smooth, elevated, grandiloquent poetic diction, and a looser, rougher, more supple, more prosaic idiom—between a more artificial order and choice of words, and a more natural one.

C. DAY LEWIS: *The Colloquial Element in English Poetry*, 1947

Every revolution in poetry is apt to be, and sometimes to announce itself as, a return to common speech. That is the revolution which Wordsworth announced in his Prefaces, and he was right: but the same revolution had been carried out a century before by Oldham, Waller, Denham and Dryden; and the same revolution was due again something over a century later. The followers of a revolution develop the new poetic idiom in one direction or another; they polish and perfect it; meanwhile the spoken language goes on changing, and the poetic idiom goes out of date. . . .

T. S. ELIOT: *The Music of Poetry*, 1942

I suppose that it will be agreed that if the work of the last twenty years is worthy of being classified at all, it is as belonging to a period of search for a proper modern colloquial idiom.

T. S. ELIOT: *The same*

◉　　◉　　◉

This does not mean, of course, an idiom which takes the colloquial exactly as it finds it. There is verse of that kind (popular with the daily press because it can so easily be disguised as prose), which is common speech at its commonest—unheightened, untouched by imagination, words used without depth or association. But this isn't poetry. It is a snapshot, not a portrait.

◉　　◉　　◉

Let the medium of poetry conform completely to the usages of ordinary speech and it ceases to be poetry. If poetry is art, it must produce
its effects through a medium which differentiates it, without divorcing
it, from reality.

JOHN LIVINGSTON LOWES

To use the language of common speech, but to employ always the *exact*
word, not the nearly-exact nor the merely decorative word.

'Imagist' manifesto. Preface to *Some Imagist Poets*, 1915

I am inclined to feel that pure colloquialism—pure slang if you like—
should be confined to poetical drama and satire. It should be directly
associated with the speech of characters in drama or in narrative. It is
felt to be unsuitable for use in lyrical or contemplative poems. Compare Shakespeare's incessant use of colloquial language in the plays,
with the complete absence of it in the sonnets.

C. DAY LEWIS, in a broadcast discussion on modern poetry, May 1935

Poetry is not the same thing as ordinary language . . . especially in its
rhythm, it makes the greatest possible appropriate use of the *sound* of
language—a much more deliberate and complex use of it than would
ever occur elsewhere. Nevertheless, the material which the poet works
in, to however elaborate a result, is the *natural* sound of living speech. . .

LASCELLES ABERCROMBIE: *Poetry: Its Music and Meaning*, 1932

No poetry, of course, is ever exactly the same speech that the poet
talks and hears; but it has to be in such a relation to the speech of his
time that the listener or reader can say, 'that is how I should talk if I
could talk poetry.' This is the reason why contemporary poetry can
give us a feeling of excitement and a sense of fulfilment different from
any sentiment aroused by even very much greater poetry of a past age.

T. S. ELIOT: *The Music of Poetry*, 1942

The first bridge to be crossed by any poet-dramatist should be the way
to reconcile his poetry to common speech, not only by the avoidance
of obvious poetical inversions and excisions, but by the method of
metaphor and simile, by the way symbolic language is presented, and

above all by the speech-rhythms, which have to overcome the tone of written literature.

CHRISTOPHER FRY: 'Poetry and the Theatre', *Adam*, 1951

There is no conversational or other form which can be applied indiscriminately: if a writer wishes to give the effect of speech he must positively give the effect of himself talking in his own person or in one of his roles; and if we are to express ourselves, our variety of thoughts and feelings, on a variety of subjects with inevitable rightness, we must adapt our manner to the moment with infinite variations. Examination of the development of Elizabethan drama shows this progress in adaptation, a development from monotony to variety, a progressive refinement in the perception of the variations of feeling, and a progressive elaboration of the means of expressing these variations.

T. S. ELIOT: 'Rhetoric and Poetic Drama', *The Sacred Wood*, 1920

❖   ❖   ❖

Poetry, too, however close it keeps to contemporary speech, must convey more than conversation. Even in drama, the poet's language does not stop short at a reproduction of everyday dialogue. While giving the illusion of reality, it must go further and express thoughts and feelings which their owners in ordinary life would leave unspoken and which they might not even know were theirs.

❖   ❖   ❖

Let us suppose the heroine of a play is emotionally, desperately, passionately anxious for the return of the hero. What, in common speech, she would say is something like 'Oh, do, do, *do* come back quickly, John!' It is not a very adequate demonstration of what her whole being is really saying. That is something much more like:

> Gallop apace, you fiery-footed steeds,
> Towards Phoebus' lodging: such a waggoner
> As Phaeton would whip you to the west
> And bring in cloudy night immediately.
> Spread thy close curtain, love-performing night!
> That runaway's eyes may wink, and Romeo
> Leap to these arms, untalked—of and unseen!

Now I do not hold this up as an example of how we should write today, or even as very fine poetry, but the passionate animation, the anticipation of night, and the feeling that there is an almost deliberate perverseness in the slowly setting sun, is an expression of truth which is absent from 'Oh, do, do, *do* come back quickly, John!' It is a great part of the poet's work to express what is unexpressed in common speech, and to use common speech to do so. . . .

CHRISTOPHER FRY: 'Poetry and the Theatre', *Adam*, 1951

A language is always changing; its development, in vocabulary, in syntax, pronunciation and intonation—even, in the long run, its deterioration—must be accepted by the poet and made the best of. He in turn has the privilege of contributing to the development and maintaining the quality, the capacity of the language to express a wide range, and subtle gradation, of feeling and emotion; his task is both to respond to change and make it conscious, and to battle against degradation below the standards which he has learnt from the past. The liberties that he may take are for the sake of order.

T. S. ELIOT: *The Music of Poetry*, 1942

❧ POETIC DICTION ❧

Poetic diction. What a forbidding, dry biscuit of a term that sounds! And what hungry generations of scholastic weevils have battened upon it!

C. DAY LEWIS, *The Colloquial Element in English Poetry*

The principal object, then, proposed in these Poems was to choose incidents and situations from common life, and to relate or describe them, throughout, as far as was possible, in a selection of language really used by men. . . . Humble and rustic life was generally chosen because, in that condition, the essential passions of the heart find a better soil in which they can attain their maturity, are less under restraint, and speak a plainer and more emphatic language. . . . The language, too, of these men has been adopted (purified indeed from what appear to be its real defects, from all lasting and rational causes of dislike or disgust) because such men hourly communicate with the best objects from which the best part of their language is originally derived; and because, from their rank in society, and the sameness and narrow circle of their intercourse, being less under the influence of social vanity, they convey their feelings and notions in simple and unelaborated expressions. Accordingly such a language, arising out of repeated experience and regular feelings, is a more permanent, and a far more philosophical language, than that which is frequently substituted for it by Poets. . . .

WILLIAM WORDSWORTH: Preface to *Lyrical Ballads*,
Third Edition, 1802

Wordsworth's doctrine is a compound of fundamental truths and subtle fallacies. And when he wrote with his eye on his theory, and not on the subject, the truths slipped out from under him, and the fallacies rode him like hags.

JOHN LIVINGSTON LOWES

Wordsworth's emphatic dogma, that the language of poetry should be the language really spoken by men, is not altogether unqualified. It should be a *selection* of such language. . . . Moreover, there is a further qualification. The language should be the real language of men in *a state of vivid sensation*.

LASCELLES ABERCROMBIE; The Art of Wordsworth, 1952

Wordsworth's theory, stripped of the limitations which he imposed upon it, was absolutely sound. The diction of poetry was to be 'a *selection* of language really used by men'. Rightly understood that means a selection of the language really used by William Wordsworth, and not of that employed by Betty Foy. The poet is more than the mouthpiece of an idiot and his mother. He is the translator of their halting speech, not a mere emulator of their inarticulateness.

JOHN LIVINGSTON LOWES: Convention and Revolt in Poetry, 1919

'The language of the middle and lower classes of society' is of course perfectly proper when you are representing dramatically the *speech* of these classes; and then no other language is proper; similarly when you are representing dramatically the language of the upper classes; but on other occasions, it is not the business of the poet to talk like *any* class of society, but like himself.

T. S. ELIOT: 'Wordsworth and Coleridge', in
The Use of Poetry, 1933

The late Sir Walter Raleigh did well to point out, apropos of Wordsworth's theory of poetic diction, that some of the flattest passages in that poet's own work are due to his having observed the *prose choice* of words (in accordance with his theory) without at the same time keeping to the natural *prose order*.

OWEN BARFIELD: Poetic Diction, 1928

It might suffice, for answering Wordsworth, to ask oneself whether 'The Ancient Mariner' could be rechristened, without loss, 'The Old Sailor'. It is surely clear that 'poetic diction' is not always bad nor yet essential; without it poetry is still possible, but as a whole would be immensely poorer.

F. L. LUCAS: The Decline and Fall of the Romantic Ideal, 1936

Nevertheless, Wordsworth performed an immense service to literature by restating the principle that poetry is an extension of common speech, not a different language, even if, in his enthusiasm for the cause, he overstated it. Indeed, it would be possible to argue that he was even more important as a leader of poetry than as a poet. (The same may be said in a hundred years' time of Mr Eliot.) Certainly it is due to him that the eighteenth-century conception of a 'poetic diction' divorced from the vocabulary and style of normal speech received—not its death-blow, because it staggered to its feet again during the nineteenth century—but at least a swashing blow that left the stage free for Coleridge, Keats, Shelley and, of course, for Wordsworth himself.

     ⊛   ⊛   ⊛

It is in the attempts of the eighteenth century to translate into its own lingo the noble simplicity of great speech, that poetic diction finds its *reductio ad absurdum*.

         JOHN LIVINGSTON LOWES

The matter and diction [of Pope] seemed to me characterized not so much by poetic thoughts, as by thoughts translated into the language of poetry.

     S. T. COLERIDGE: *Biographia Literaria*, 1817

One great distinction I appeared to see plainly between even the characteristic faults of our elder poets, and the false beauty of the moderns. In the former, from Donne to Cowley, we find the most fantastic out-of-the-way thoughts, but in the most pure and genuine mother English—in the latter the most obvious thoughts, in language the most fantastic and arbitrary.

     S. T. COLERIDGE: *Biographia Literaria*, 1817

[Writing of Samuel Rogers' verse]: This kind of poetry . . . is like the game of asking what one's thoughts are like. It is a tortuous, tottering, wriggling, fidgetty translation of everything from the vulgar tongue into all the tantalising, teasy, tripping, lisping *mimminee-pimminee* of the highest brilliancy and fashion of poetical diction.

   WILLIAM HAZLITT:'On the Living Poets' from
       Lectures on the English Poets, 1818

... Natural language, neither bookish nor vulgar, neither redolent of the lamp nor of the kennel—such as 'I will remember thee', instead of the same thought tricked up in the rag-fair finery of

> —thy image on her wing
> Before my fancy's eye shall memory bring.

S. T. COLERIDGE: *Biographia Literaria*, 1817

Words once nobly used were taken by the Romantics' successors to be inherently noble, and were employed to confer on poetry the nobility which it is poetry's function to confer on words.

JOHN LIVINGSTON LOWES

If the creative energy is strong enough, the most intractable words may be merged ... into the very stuff of poetry.

JOHN LIVINGSTON LOWES

Ugly words are the words not fitted to the company in which they find themselves.

T. S. ELIOT

There are misguided souls who think that a word like 'scratch', for example, is unpoetic. In splendid isolation, I suppose it is. But in poetry that is worthy of the name there are no isolated words. Their suggestions interpenetrate each other, and every word—even 'scratch' —may take on, chameleon-like, the colours of its fellows.

> Then a mile of warm sea-scented beach;
> Three fields to cross till a farm appears;
> A tap at the pane, the quick sharp scratch
> And blue spurt of a lighted match,
> And a voice less loud, through its joys and fears,
> Than the two hearts beating each to each.

If the current runs strong, there are few words which it cannot safely carry with it.

JOHN LIVINGSTON LOWES: *Convention and Revolt in Poetry*, 1919

Imagination can use the simplest diction, because it has got at the truth, found what can appeal to the right mind of man, because it is strong

in life, thought and language. Rich poetic vocabulary is then un-
necessary. Such simple poems as Drayton's sonnet,

Since there's no help, come, let us kiss and part,

and Herrick's lines,

Now is the time when all the lights wax dim,

are full of meaning, of stress, of 'passion'—to use Milton's term.
Passages like those are good to remember as touchstones of poetic
diction, to test the depth of the rich language of the ornamental poets.

W. P. KER: *Form and Style in Poetry*, 1929

The line about the sea which 'moans round with many voices', a true
specimen of Tennyson-Virgilianism, is too *poetical*, in comparison with
Dante, to be the highest poetry. Only Shakespeare can be so 'poetical'
without giving any effect of overloading, or distracting us from the
main issue:

Put up your bright swords or the dew will rust them.

T. S. ELIOT: *Dante*, 1929

His [Shakespeare's] metaphors, when extracted and examined apart
from their context, are found to contain the most definite, concrete,
and often un-'poetical' words: but his imagination worked at so high
a temperature that no object, however solid, angular and tough, failed
to be fused into the material texture of his poetry.

C. DAY LEWIS: *A Hope for Poetry*, 1936

The eldest of the present, and the newest of the past language, is the
best.   BEN JONSON

Peculiar, not far-fetched; natural, but not obvious; delicate, not
affected; dignified, not swelling; fiery, but not mad; rich in imagery,
but not loaded with it—in short, a union of harmony and good sense,
of perspicuity and conciseness.

S. T. COLERIDGE: *Anima Poetæ*, 1797–1801

Each age laboriously creates its own poetic language and style and then
destroys it. Words and images become so thumbed and slobbered over

N

that they are blurred and vague. The reader becomes immune to them as he does to a laxative. . . . When poetry reaches this stage—and it happens periodically in literature—it is necessary to de-poetise it. In our century, Eliot has been the chief agent in this work.

NORMAN NICHOLSON: *Outposts*, No. 5, 1945

The true poetic conception must find its own language, and that language must be such as to convey, not particular fragmentary beauties, but the whole poetic idea, the emotional and imaginative creature of the mind, with no distraction or encumbrance.

W. P. KER: 'William Wordsworth',
Chambers' Cyclopaedia of Literature

✤ PROSE AND POETRY ✤

Prose is the museum where the dead metaphors of the past are preserved.

T. E. HULME

Poetry may be poetry . . . and the loftiest at that, without employing the diction which we call poetic. Its richest store lies within and not without the tract that it holds in common with prose.

JOHN LIVINGSTON LOWES

. . . that a poet ever uses a word as poetical—that is, formally—which he, in the same mood and thought, would not use in prose or conversation, Milton's prose works will assist us in disproving. . . . Poetry demands a severe keeping. It admits nothing that prose may not often admit, but it oftener rejects. In other words, it presupposes a more continuous state of passion.
S. T. COLERIDGE: *Anima Poetæ*, 1805

◉   ◉   ◉

If poetry moves too far away from the prose of its time, it drifts into song, where the music is more important than the meaning. If it approaches too close to prose, it ceases to move us in the way we expect verse to move us: it tends to come under the dominance of the logical, reasoning part of the brain. It has no 'overtones', no imaginative suggestiveness.

◉   ◉   ◉

. . . Poetry has as much to learn from prose as from other poetry; and I think that an interaction between prose and verse, like the interaction between language and language, is a condition of vitality in literature.

T. S. ELIOT: Conclusion to *The Use of Poetry*, 1933

Hardly any good poet in English has written *bad* prose; and some English poets have been among the greatest of English prose writers.

T. S. ELIOT: Introduction 1930 to Samuel Johnson's *London*

Just as, from *Wuthering Heights* and *Moby Dick* to the work of James Joyce and Virginia Woolf, novelists can be seen enriching fiction with the symbolism and the heightened language which used to be considered the preserve of poetry, so in the last thirty years poetry has tended towards the language of prose and of every-day conversation; tended to become more colloquial in expression, and to follow more closely the rhythms of ordinary speech.

C. DAY LEWIS: Broadcast talk, 'Techniques in
Modern Poetry', February 1953

Poetry has always striven to be something other than prose. Wordsworth and Coleridge had their strong views on the border-line between the two. Modern poetry is facing the same problem by taking speech, when it is the language of men in a state of excitement, and making certain that that excitement lifts it above prose. There is a danger that the excitement may not be communicated. Wordsworth's contemporaries were not yet attuned, and often thought his verse prose.[1]

J. ISAACS: *The Background of Modern Poetry*, 1951

... the difference between poetry and prose is decided by the direction of language, more than by analysing the prose into its poetic elements. Prose is language used in such a way that the ideas and events or scenes within the language are referred to as objects existing apart from the language, so that there is an understanding between the writer and the reader that these things could be discussed in quite other words than those used, because they exist independently of the words. But directly the language tends to create, as it were, verbal objects inseparable from the words used, then the direction of the language is poetic. It is moving towards a condition where, as in poetry, the words appear to become the object, so that they cannot be replaced by other words than the ones used to convey the same experience.

STEPHEN SPENDER: *World within World*, 1951

---

[1] Sometimes, of course, they were not far wrong!

❧ RHYTHM AND METRE ❧

*There is something magical about rhythm: it even makes us
believe that the sublime lies within our reach.*

GOETHE

It is this movement, this orderly movement, that gives to every poem,
every poetic passage, its specific character—I might say, its vital
heart-beat.

STANLEY LEATHES: *Rhythm in English Poetry*, 1935

Rhythm acts like a flywheel which both increases power and regu-
lates it.

P. GURREY

The moment the drums stop beating, the function of art ceases.

WYNDHAM LEWIS

Metre, like the beating of a tom-tom, seems actually to be a means of
exciting yet hypnotizing the hearer, so that he is both spell-bound like
the Mariner's Wedding-guest, and at the same time more suggestible
to whatever he is told.

F. L. LUCAS: footnote to *Decline and Fall of
the Romantic Ideal*, 1936

Now the exciting power of rhythm is well known: the beating of
drums is an instance. But it is also well known that a too monotonous
rhythm, after the first excitement of it has passed, becomes deadening,
like drugs that stimulate at first, and then stupify. The metre of poetry,
however, consists essentially of two elements: an element of constancy
and an element of variation, the pattern and its modulations. By the
repeating pattern of his rhythm the poet can give his reader's mind the
right sort of excitement for the receiving of his subject; but by the
continual modulations of the pattern he can prevent the rhythm from

becoming monotonous and stupefying: he can keep its action on the mind always fresh and effective.

LASCELLES ABERCROMBIE: *Poetry: Its Music and Meaning*, 1932

The purpose of rhythm, it has always seemed to me, is to prolong the moment of contemplation, the moment when we are both asleep and awake, which is the one moment of creation, by hushing us with an alluring monotony, while it holds us waking by variety, to keep us in the state of perhaps real trance, in which the mind liberated from the pressure of the will is unfolded in symbols.

W. B. YEATS: *Autobiographies*, 1926

Poetry is a very vital thing. It draws its metaphors from ordinary life, and it draws its rhythms from ordinary speech. But emotion demands a greater regularity of rhythm than we expect or desire in our non-emotional moods.

F. H. HAYWARD: *The Lesson in Appreciation*, 1922

The language of elevated thought or feeling is always rhythmic. Strong feeling of whatever sort, that is, imposes upon speech a rhythmic beat. Even you and I, whose ordinary daily talk maintains its slow or hurried, nervous or phlegmatic, staccato or legato, but always pedestrian gait— even you and I, under stress of compelling emotion, find our speech taking on not only deeper colour, but a more or less measured beat.

JOHN LIVINGSTON LOWES: *Convention and Revolt in Poetry*, 1919

The poet, it is true, introduces a more regular rhythm into his poetry than a prose writer introduces into his prose, but the regularity is fitful and unobtrusive; thought and its natural expression are his main concern, and he is a great poet if he can so shape his words as just to suggest regularity and recurrence, and at the same time not to betray in the slightest the everyday genius of the language.

F. H. HAYWARD: *The Lesson in Appreciation*, 1922

◉   ◉   ◉

It is at this point that confusion usually arises between 'poetic rhythm' and 'metre', especially as so many people, including critics, employ these terms as if they were synonymous. Yet an understanding of their difference, and a realization of where that difference lies, seems to me basic to poetic appreciation. So much potential enjoyment has been killed by trying to understand poetry from the wrong end—from a study of so-called 'metrical systems', instead of from the root of poetry which is common speech.

In recent years, phoneticians have made important discoveries relating to the natural laws of spoken English which the literary critic has largely ignored. Among these is the fact that stress in English conversation tends towards regularity—not the machine-gun precision of French, but a more varied, flexible regularity dependent to a large extent on the unconscious manipulation of unstressed syllables. Something in the nature of the speaker encourages him to alter the vowel-values and the rate of speaking so that a fairly even accentuation is maintained, while in between the stresses dance an irregular number of unstressed syllables. It is the Englishman's desire for compromise, and his delight in ordered idiosyncrasy, revealed through language. If several unstressed syllables occur between one stressed syllable and the next, he weakens and hurries them so as not to delay the next stress too much; if two stressed syllables come together, he spaces them out so that the accentuation is not too rapid.[1] In this way there has developed a wonderful range of speech-rhythms, instinctive and native to the language. English is naturally rhythmic, beautiful in itself and at the same time ideal for the composition of poetry.

Normally, of course, there is only this *tendency* to regularity, which produces rhythm though not necessarily poetic rhythm. But when the speaker is emotionally affected, as Professor Lowes has suggested, the rhythm becomes more pronounced and speech moves spontaneously towards verse. The poet, sensing the underlying urge to regularity, often brings it closer to the surface, so tightening and heightening the accentuation that a pattern is recognized which remains more or less constant throughout the poem. Even then, however, in any poem worth the name, the pattern is never mechanical. A norm is found round which the natural rhythms of speech move with more than usual certainty. The norm is 'metre'; the final result of the interweaving of speech-rhythms round the norm is 'poetic rhythm'. But—and this is supremely important—the rhythm comes to the writer first, as an instinctive accompaniment to the thought or feeling. He doesn't start deliberately from the other end and work out his rhythms by skilful avoidances of the norm, as so many textbooks imply. It is only afterwards that the metre is analysed—by those who wish to analyse. What

[1] See *An Outline of English Phonetics* by Daniel Jones, and *The Phonetics of English* by I. Ward (Heffer and Sons, Cambridge).

we are apt to forget, however, is that a whole galaxy of different rhythms can move round the same norm. To read the average text-book one would imagine that poets were confined to about half a dozen. As Virginia Woolf once said, a lover of poetry with a good ear can learn more than a professor with a measuring-rod.

*   *   *

At school we generally learn about metre only—to 'scan' verses—and this is so dull that we seldom go farther to enjoy the real beauties of rhythm. To see a class studying a poem and working out the metre with a loud *ke-bonk*, *ke-bonk* of a pencil on the desk is a most depressing sight. If poetry really moves in this wooden-legged swing, it is not surprising that many sensible people do not like it; ordinary speech is so much more varied, subtle and interesting!

MARJORIE BOULTON: *The Anatomy of Poetry*, 1953

It is most unfortunate that many people have had so narrow a concept of 'rhythm' forced upon them that they feel a poem 'does not scan' if it contains variations, and they try to force it into unnatural, ugly rhythms if it is the work of an acknowledged master, or condemn it as incompetent if it is by a poet unlucky enough to be still alive.

MARJORIE BOULTON: *The same*

The passage seems to be a rotten sonnet, written in a very tempera-mental kind of iambic pentameter. Not even by cruel forcing and beating the table with my fingers can I find the customary five iambic feet to the verse.

Student-critic on Donne's sonnet, 'At the round earth's imagined corners'. Quoted by Dr I. A. Richards in *Practical Criticism*, 1929

Count and balance syllables, work out an addition of the feet in the verse by a foot-rule, and you will seem to have traced every miracle back to its root in a natural product. Only something, that is every-thing, will have escaped you. As well dissect a corpse to find out the principles of life.

ARTHUR SYMONS

Metre can be reckoned, rhythm can only be felt.

STANLEY LEATHES: *Rhythm in English Poetry*, 1935

When I say that the rhythm of poetry is regular, I do not mean that it is always the same. It is like the rise and fall of the sea rather than the pendulum of a clock.

P. H. B. LYON: *The Discovery of Poetry*, 1930

Rhythm is a continual endangering and retrieving of balance.[1]

ALLAN KEELING

The temporal recurrences of rhythm are never identical, as the metrical notation would seem to suggest. Rhythm is to time what symmetry is to space. Seen from a certain distance, the features of a human face seem symmetrically arranged and constant in size and position. . . . Close up, however, the regularity disappears; the size and position of the features varies slightly from face and face and, indeed, if a face could exist in which the symmetry was mathematically perfect, it would appear not a face, but a lifeless mask.

W. H. AUDEN: 'The Poetic Process', B.B.C. Talk, June 1956

There is in verse, on the one hand, the metrical unit—that is to say, for our present purpose, the line. There is, on the other hand, what we may designate as the sentence rhythm or cadence. If the line-length and the sentence rhythm uniformly coincide (as they do in some of Pope's couplets, for example) we get monotony, deadly and intolerable. If there is only the sentence cadence, without the beat of the line, there is variety, but it is merely the variety of your speech and mine, when charged with emotion in varying degrees. Metrical verse, that is not sheer doggerel, is built upon the harmony of both. Behind the end-lessly weaving rhythms of the sentence cadences beats steadily, in the best verse unobtrusively, the rhythm of the line. In the hands of the artist, the rhythmic cadences determined by the thought, or by the breath, or both, flow around and through and in the best of the lines, but the beat of the lines is *there*, like time in music.

JOHN LIVINGSTON LOWES: *Convention and Revolt in Poetry*, 1919

One of the things that please the ear when we listen to a poem being read aloud is the contrast, the sort of friendly wrestle between its metre and its speech-rhythm; the metre is like a tide pulsing regularly

[1] Metre the tight-rope, rhythm the walker.

underneath, the speech-rhythm is a less regular movement, like ripples on the surface.

C. DAY LEWIS: *Poetry for You*, 1944

This texture of expectations, satisfactions, disappointments, surprisals, which the sequence of syllables brings about, is rhythm. . . . Evidently there can be no surprise and no disappointment unless there is expectation, and most rhythms perhaps are made up as much of disappointments and postponements and surprises and betrayals as of simple, straightforward satisfactions. Hence the rapidity with which too-simple rhythms, those which are too easily seen 'through', grow cloying or insipid. . . .

I. A. RICHARDS: *Principles of Literary Criticism*, 1924

We enjoy going for a walk along the same lane many times; but, while part of the pleasure is in the familiarity, part lies in the new discoveries at different seasons and in different weathers.

MARJORIE BOULTON: *The Anatomy of Poetry*, 1953

The pattern [of metre] is only a convenience, though an invaluable one; it indicates the *general* movement of the rhythm; it gives a model, a central line, from which variations in the movement take their direction and gain an added significance; it gives both poet and reader a firm support, a fixed point of orientation in the indefinitely vast world of possible rhythms. . . .

I. A. RICHARDS: *Practical Criticism*, 1929

SPRUNG RHYTHM ❧
& SPRINGLESS

Read it with the ears, as it was meant to be read, and then my
verse is all right.
GERARD MANLEY HOPKINS to Robert Bridges

We have seen how the rhythmical quality of the English language is always seeking order without the sacrifice of variety. It was on this native habit of speech, including our unconscious manipulation of unstressed syllables, that Hopkins based his theory of 'sprung rhythm'. His confined life made this appear to him far more complicated than it really was; for, as he himself pointed out, he was only doing in practice what Chaucer, Wyatt and even the anonymous writers of nursery rhymes had done centuries before.

❦   ❦   ❦

I had long had haunting my ear the echo of a new rhythm which I now realized on paper. To speak shortly, it consists in scanning by accents or stresses alone, without any account of the number of syllables, so that a foot may be one strong syllable or it may be many light and one strong. I do not say the idea is altogether new: there are hints of it in music,[1] in nursery rhymes and popular jingles, in the poets themselves. . . . But no one has professedly used it and made it the principle throughout, that I know of. Nevertheless to me it appears, I own, to be a better and more natural principle than the ordinary system, much more flexible, and capable of much greater effects.

GERARD MANLEY HOPKINS in a letter to
R. W. Dixon, 5 October 1878

Why do I employ sprung rhythm at all? Because it is the nearest to the rhythm of prose, that is the native and natural rhythm of speech,

[1] Plain-song, for instance.

the least forced, the most rhetorical and emphatic of all possible rhythms, combining, as it seems to me, opposite and, one would have thought, incompatible excellences, markedness of rhythm—that is rhythm's self—and naturalness of expression—for why, if it is forcible in prose to say 'láshed ród' am I obliged to weaken this in verse, which ought to be stronger, not weaker, into 'láshed birch-rod' or something? My verse is less to be read than heard, as I have told you before. . . .

GERARD MANLEY HOPKINS: 21 August, 1877, *Letters to Robert Bridges*

*   *   *

Hopkins would never have needed to advance it as a theory at all if so many poets and critics of the eighteenth and nineteenth centuries, from Dryden to Robert Bridges, had not weakened the natural resources of the language by their misapplied learning. For one disastrous result of the Renaissance was that it not only brought Englishmen in contact with literature of other countries and other times, but it gave the comparatively few who could study it in the original an exaggerated view of its (and their own) importance. Instead of seeing Greek poetry as a development of Greek speech, and Latin poetry of the Latin, they imagined that the laws governing these foreign literatures could be artificially grafted onto English. We have been suffering from the results of this attitude for the last two hundred years in the 'systems' on which so many scholars have insisted that English poetry is written. They have collected a mere handful of metres, with foreign labels, and tried to compress the hundreds of English rhythms into their mould, explaining all square pegs and misfits by the terms 'resolutions', 'inversions' and 'poetic licence'.

It is true that poetry has flourished in spite of the metrists. But how many thousands of potential readers have been turned against it, and how many potentially great poets like Pope have allowed their gifts to be put into strait-jackets? One has only to open some school text-books today to see that this eighteenth-century attitude is not defeated yet.

*   *   *

It is remarkable that when art grew thoroughly self-conscious in the eighteenth century, and men became emphatically aware of rhythm as a discrete entity, only the very simplest rhythms were felt as rhythmic. The eighteenth-century found the complex rhythms of earlier ages too difficult.

KATHARINE M. WILSON: *Sound and Meaning in English Poetry*, 1930

They swayed about upon a rocking horse,
And thought it Pegasus.

JOHN KEATS: *Sleep and Poetry*, 1817

I know that the ears of modern verse-writers are delicate to an excess, and their readers are troubled with the same squeamishness as themselves. So that if a line do not run as smooth as quicksilver, they are offended. A critic of the present day serves a poem as a cook serves a dead turkey, when she fastens the legs of it to a post, and draws out all the sinews. For this we may thank Pope; but unless we could imitate him in the closeness and compactness of his expression, as well as in the smoothness of his numbers, we had better drop the imitation, which serves no other purpose than to emasculate and weaken all we write. Give me a manly rough line, with a deal of meaning in it, rather than a whole poem full of musical periods that have nothing but their oily smoothness to recommend them! . . . There is a roughness on a plum, which nobody that understands fruit would rub off, though the plum would be much more polished without it.

WILLIAM COWPER in a letter to John Johnson, 1791

Since Dryden, the metre of our poets leads to the sense; in our elder and more genuine bards, the sense, including the passion, leads to the metre.

S. T. COLERIDGE: Lecture on Beaumont and Fletcher, 1818

I count by Beats or accents instead of syllables—in the belief that a metre might be thus produced sufficiently uniform and far more malleable to the Passion and Meaning.

S. T. COLERIDGE in a letter to Byron on 'Christabel', 1815

Rhythm must have meaning. It can't be merely a careless dash off, with no grip and no real hold to the words and sense, a *tumpty tum tumpty tum tum ta*.

EZRA POUND: *Letters*, 1951

The rhythm which we admire, which we seem to detect actually *in* the sounds, and which we seem to respond to, is something we only *ascribe* to them and is, actually, a rhythm of the mental activity through which we apprehend not only the sound of the words but their sense and feeling. The mysterious glory which seems to inhere in the sound of certain lines is a projection of the thought and emotion they evoke, and the peculiar satisfaction they seem to give *to the ear* is a reflection of the adjustment *of our feelings* which has been momentarily achieved.

I. A. RICHARDS: *Practical Criticism*, 1929

In Massinger, as in all our poets before Dryden, in order to make harmonious verse in the reading, it is absolutely necessary that the meaning should be understood—when the meaning is once seen, then the harmony is perfect. Whereas in Pope, and in most of the writers who followed in his school, it is the mechanical metre which determines the sense.

S. T. COLERIDGE: Lecture on Massinger, 1818

[In Chaucer] every foot beats time to the tune of thought.

J. R. LOWELL: *Chaucer*, 1870

In [Shakespeare] the beat in the rhythm is the pulse of the thought itself.

HERBERT READ

His rhythm is so perfect that you may be almost sure that you do not understand the real force of a line if it does not run well as you read it.

S. T. COLERIDGE: *Table Talk*, 12 May 1830

Schiller's blank verse is bad. He moves in it as a fly in a glue-bottle. His thoughts have their connection and variety, it is true, but there is no sufficiently corresponding movement in the verse. How different from Shakespeare's endless rhythms!

S. T. COLERIDGE: *Table Talk*, 2 June 1834

In some of Swinburne's poetry the metre seems to dictate the thought. The mind simply relaxes and is carried along on the wave of sound. It is a kind of poetic surf-riding.

CLIVE SANSOM

The rhythm of poetry . . . is really the rhythm of our *thinking* when we are reading the words of a poem; and not only of our thinking, but of the accompanying activities of perception, imagination and intuition.

P. GURREY: *The Appreciation of Poetry*, 1935

It is true that quantity, an almost iron law with the Greeks is, in English, rather a subject for a peculiarly fine ear, than any law or even rule; but then, instead of it, we have, first, accent; secondly, emphasis; and lastly, retardation and acceleration of the times of the syllables, according to the meaning of the words, the passion that accompanies them, and even the character of the person that uses them.

S. T. COLERIDGE: Lecture on Massinger, 1818

For rhythm is no matter of tricks with syllables, but directly reflects personality. It is not separable from the words to which it belongs. Moving rhythm in poetry arises only from genuinely stirred impulses, and is a more subtle index than any other to the order of the interests.[1]

I. A. RICHARDS: *Science and Poetry*, 1935

Milton and Shakespeare possibly did not know how complex were the designs of their rhythms; their command of rhythmic composition was intuitional, half-conscious. They wrote more from a general sense of music than from particularized feeling for the design of their rhythms.

KATHARINE M. WILSON: *Sound and Meaning in English Poetry*, 1930

It is inconceivable that he [Shakespeare] can have intended these lines to be read so that they contained five feet, each with a stress on the second syllable, with an occasional 'inversion' or 'resolution'. Rather we can imagine him saying: 'Yes, there are about ten syllables in each of my lines. I know that there are stresses and quantities; I dispose them as I think best, in order to suit the rhythm, quality, texture and music of my words. The order, position and succession of stresses and quantities hover around a norm, but are seldom identical with that norm. The total effect is the product of my art, which I could not even myself reduce to law. If you don't like my ways, and think I ought to be more

---

[1] 'Moving rhythm' is a most useful phrase, because it is the dynamic quality of rhythm which ultimately differentiates it from metre (or inorganic rhythm) which is static.

orderly, I am sorry; but I feel that our English language is very flexible, and I believe that it will stand a good deal of pulling about. I simply could not begin to write if there were some pedant who prescribed the rules by which I should work.'

STANLEY LEATHES: *Rhythm in English Poetry*, 1935

All this [the study of metre] need scarcely be known as a preparation either for writing or reading English verse. The poet has only to arrange his words so that the accents will recur at like intervals, and very few for whom he writes will fail to recognize the character of his rhythm, and to measure it off correctly in their reading. It is true that, if unusual measures are used, it may be necessary to put long words, or those in which the accent is unmistakable, at the beginning of the first line or two, but the clue once given, the rhythm will take care of itself. The smallest children, able to talk, catch with ease the movements of Mother Goose's melodies, some of which contain metres as complicated as are ever constructed.

GEORGE LANSING RAYMOND: *Poetry as a Representative Art*, 1899

It is highly probable that the Greeks would have given a very poor metrical account of the very complex choruses of their tragedies. And certainly the Elizabethan audience would not make much of the metre of late Shakespeare. But—this is what matters—the choruses sounded good to the Greeks, and the late Shakespearean rhythm sounded good to the Elizabethans. And as long as the rhythm of modern poetry sounds all right, there is surely little reason to complain that we cannot analyse it.

HUGH SYKES DAVIES: Broadcast Talk on
Modern Poetry, September 1933

If one thought about it while making a poem, one would go mad and produce nothing of value.

J. W. GOETHE: *Conversations with Eckermann*, 6 April 1829

It often seems to me as though an invisible genius were whispering something rhythmical to me, so that on my walks I always keep step to it, and at the same time I fancy I hear soft tones accompanying some song, which then comes to me in one way or another and delights me.

Wilhelm in GOETHE's Die Wanderjahre, quoted in
The Anatomy of Inspiration

Rhythm . . . and the connection between metre and rhythm, are strange and mysterious forces. Those who best understand their power are often the most reluctant to attempt explanations. A classic example of this hesitation was provided in an unexpected quarter by the famous jazz-pianist 'Fats' Waller. In reply to one who had asked him what rhythm was, that courteous but unconventional son of the manse replied: 'Lady, if you has to ask, you ain't got it.'

Reviewer of Catherine Ing's *Elizabethan Lyrics*
in *The Times Literary Supplement*

❧ FREE VERSE ❧

Vers libre *is exploring the borderland between prose and verse.*
J. LIVINGSTON LOWES

With most verse, then, poetic rhythm is the result of a compromise between the speech rhythm and an underlying, though often unconscious, metrical norm. But it is possible to take over the phrasing, rhythms and cadences of speech, and by heightening them without using any analysible metre, to create rhythms that are unquestionably poetic. The James I translations of the Psalms proved this; so, at their luckiest moments, have Whitman, D. H. Lawrence and Ezra Pound.

By choosing so-called 'free verse' these writers have denied themselves one of the most potent means of stimulating and at the same time controlling poetic emotion. Also by refusing a guide, their foot often slips and they fall flat into prose. But when it 'comes off', the result can have a uniquely satisfying quality, right in its place and belonging to no other poem. Pound's,

> The paired butterflies are already yellow with August
> Over the grass in the west garden . . .

is rhythmically perfect and in its context as genuinely poetic as the touchstone line of Keats:

> I cannot see what flowers are at my feet.

But the writer of free verse (and his reader) needs a very sensitive ear.

❀　　❀　　❀

As regards his free verse, I—plus some chianti—once put forward the old notion that free verse was like fishing with barbless hooks. Henley replied volcanically. It was, said he, 'the cadences that did it.'

RUDYARD KIPLING: *Something of Myself*, 1937

Vers libre is built upon 'organic rhythm' or the rhythm of the speaking voice with its necessity for breathing, rather than upon a strict metrical system.

AMY LOWELL: 'Tendencies in Modern American
Poetry', *The Dial*, 17 January 1918

I think more of a bird with broad wings, flying and lapsing through the air, than anything, when I think of metre[1]. . . . It all depends on the *pause*, the natural pause, the natural lingering of the voice according to the feeling—it is the hidden emotional pattern that makes poetry, not the obvious form.

D. H. LAWRENCE: *Letters*

Only a bad poet could welcome free verse as a liberation from form. It was a revolt against dead form, and a preparation for a new form or for the renewal of the old; it was an insistence upon the inner unity which is unique to every poem, against the outer unity which is typical.

T. S. ELIOT: *The Music of Poetry*, 1942

No *vers* is *libre* for the man who wants to do a good job.

T. S. ELIOT: Introduction to Ezra Pound's *Poems*, 1940

One should write *vers libre* only when one must; that is to say, only when the 'thing' builds up a rhythm more beautiful than that of set metres, or more real, more a part of the emotion of the 'thing', more germane, intimate, interpretative than the measure of regular accentual verse.

EZRA POUND: *Literary Essays*, 1954

The ghost of some simple metre should lurk behind the arras in the freest verse, to advance menacingly as we doze and withdraw as we rouse.

T. S. ELIOT

Even Browning's verse always goes to a recognizable tune (I say not to a good one), but in the name of all bagpipes, what is the tune of Emerson's?

A. C. SWINBURNE in a letter to Edmund Stedman,
20 February 1875

[1] He obviously intended the word 'rhythm' here.

 RHYME

*It is already sayde (and, as I think, trulie sayde) it is not
ryming and versing that maketh Poesie.*
SIR PHILIP SIDNEY, *An Apologie for Poetrie*

Rhyme is chiefly used to link lines together into those larger masses of
continuous rhythm which the metres of individual lines exist to create.
. . . The function of rhyme is thus primarily structural.

LASCELLES ABERCROMBIE: *Poetry: Its Music and Meaning,* 1932

. . . rhyme is sometimes considered an artificial or exotic ornament of
verse. Though sea-anemones make the beds of the sea beautiful,
scientists do not think of them as frills oversewn onto the garment of
the universe, and no more are the echoes of poetry frills.

KATHARINE M. WILSON: *Sound and Meaning in English Poetry,* 1930

It is probably true, even of the best writers, that

> Rimes the rudders are of verses
> By which, like ships, they steer their courses,

but most people's first voyages, in command, are made in vessels that
are all rudder, and they frequently retire from the trade before this
stage has been passed. An exaggerated respect for rhyming ability is
the result, and a tendency to great severity towards verses in which the
poet, if concerned only with making his rhymes perfect, could be
charged with partial unsuccess. That the poet may have had other,
more difficult and more important, tasks in hand is easily overlooked.
And that he could possibly have *intended* only a partial rhyme, and
have preferred it to a full one, is too bewildering a thought to be
entertained.

I. A. RICHARDS: *Practical Criticism,* 1929

Many poets so think in rhyme that we can say neither that the rhyme came first nor that the thought came first, but that their thought came in rhymed form.

KATHARINE M. WILSON: *Sound and Meaning in English Poetry*, 1930

*The only thing that can be successfully
translated is a Bishop.*
SYDNEY SMITH

. . . whatever lines can be translated into other words of the same
language, without diminution of their significance, either in sense or
association, or in any worthy feeling, are so far vicious in their diction.

s. t. coleridge: *Biographia Literaria*, 1817

⊛   ⊛   ⊛

That is why paraphrase is impossible. The better the poem, the more
futile the attempt, the more obvious the failure. Poetry is not prose in
fancy dress. In fact, if a poem can be expressed in prose the writing
(and the reading) of it has been a sheer waste of time. For the 'meaning'
of a poem is not any literal prose meaning which may seem to be there
from a superficial reading with the eye alone. It is the total effect on the
ear and mind and emotions of all the words, in the order in which they
have been arranged, with all their sounds, rhythms, associations and
overtones. That is to say, the one meaning possible to extract from a
poem is the poem itself.

⊛   ⊛   ⊛

. . . in true poetry it is, in strictness, impossible to express the meaning
in any but its own words, or to change the words without changing
the meaning. A translation of such poetry is not really the old meaning
in a new dress; it is a new product, something like the poem, though, if
one chooses to say so, more like it in the aspect of meaning than in the
aspect of form.

a. c. bradley: *Oxford Lectures on Poetry*, 1909

The language of poets has ever affected a certain uniform and harmonious recurrence of sound, without which it were not poetry, and
which is scarcely less indispensable to the communication of its influence than the words themselves. . . . Hence the vanity of trans-

lation; it were as wise to cast a violet into a crucible that you might discover the formal principle of its colour and odour, as seek to transfuse from one language into another the creations of a poet. The plant must spring again from its seed, or it will bear no flower. . . .

P. B. SHELLEY: A Defence of Poetry, 1820

❀   ❀   ❀

The 'best' translations, in the sense of being the most literal and exact, are not necessarily the best as poetry. Scholars have criticized Fitzgerald's 'Omar Khayyam' and Pound's translations from the Chinese, yet in each case the poet has succeeded in producing something that is acceptable as poetry in its own right. He has, as it were, brought the original poet to an English-speaking country and encouraged him to write a new poem in the new language. To one reader at least, this seems as much as we can expect. It is far more satisfying than those versions where, instead of a fresh plant growing organically from seed, the translator has assembled accurate reproductions of its petals and stuck them together with glue.

❀   ❀   ❀

It is indeed impossible to translate poetry, in the sense of finding a precise equivalent to poetical language. But it is none the less possible to be inspired to write fine native verse by the inspiration of fine foreign verse.

G. K. CHESTERTON: Chaucer, 1932

❦ WORDS ❦

I look upon fine Phrases like a Lover.
JOHN KEATS in a letter to Benjamin Bailey

. . . that long series of love-affairs with Words which is the poet's working life, and wherein Thought must play the delicate dual role of chaperone and pandar. . . .

C. DAY LEWIS: *The Poet's Task*, 1951

I was asked lately why so many people are afraid of poetry. I said it was because poetry uses words at their strongest. The everyday use of words, in the press, in conversation, in letters, is so weak. Let me put it in this way. Take two tumblers. In one put a finger of gin and fill to the brim with water; that is your everyday use of words. Fill the other to the brim with neat gin—no, I do not mean that poetry is a violent intoxicant—I mean this: superficially, both tumblers look exactly alike. And many people are cross when they find they are not alike, that poetry is simply too strong for them. It looks all right, but suddenly you find yourself involved, stirred to the roots; it is a shock. And we don't like shocks.

PATRIC DICKINSON: Broadcast talk,
The Listener, 23 July 1953

Poetry . . . sweeps the chords of all the faculties that we possess. When it is forthright, it deals in forthright words; when thought plays glancing and shifting above the deeper current, its diction becomes prismatic and subtle with intellectual quality; when it runs through the whole gamut, then, as Coleridge has it, 'words that convey feelings, and words that flash images, and words of abstract notion, flow together, and rush on like a stream.'

JOHN LIVINGSTON LOWES: *Convention and Revolt in Poetry*, 1919

. . . It is not the quantity of words a writer has at his disposal, but the way in which he disposes them that gives him his rank as a poet. His sense of how they modify each other, how their separate effects in the mind combine, how they fit into the whole response, is what matters.

I. A. RICHARDS: *Science and Poetry*, 1935

The chief characteristic of poets is their amazing *command* of words.

I. A. RICHARDS

The poet, from the start, is a man playing with words, fascinated, obsessed by them. As he gains mastery over them, he makes the game increasingly more difficult for himself, partly by inventing new rules, breaking away from the traditional techniques in which his juvenilia were written, attempting more subtle or daring combinations of words: partly because his experience has become richer and more complex, thus demanding of him greater verbal efforts to get at the truth of it.

C. DAY LEWIS: *The Poet's Task*, 1951

In the truly great poets, he [James Bowyer] would say, there is a reason assignable, not only for every word, but for the position of every word; and I well remember that, availing himself of the synonyms to the Homer of Didymus, he made us attempt to show, with regard to each, why it would not have answered the same purpose; and therein consisted the peculiar fitness of the word in the original text.

S. T. COLERIDGE: *Biographia Literaria*, 1817

Now there are people who imagine, because we all use words, whereas only few of us make any pretence of using colours or playing instruments, that therefore it must be easier to write great literature than to paint great pictures or compose great music. Don't you believe it! It is of course easier for us to write than to paint or make up tunes, but to write *well* —that is a very different affair. I am not sure that it is not in a sense harder to use words properly than other materials, simply because we are so familiar with them. We come very quickly to lose a sense of their values, we can no longer distinguish subtle shades of meaning or know good words from bad. The good writer is a man who has preserved his 'taste' for words, and who has the judgment to choose exactly the ones he requires.

P. H. B. LYON: *The Discovery of Poetry*, 1930

William tired himself with seeking an epithet for the cuckoo.

DOROTHY WORDSWORTH: *Journals*

For some time I have been trying to find the right word for the shim-mering glancing twinkling movement of the poplar-leaves in the sun and wind. This afternoon I saw the word written on the poplar-leaves. It was 'dazzle'. The dazzle of the poplars.

FRANCIS KILVERT: *Diary*, 7 October 1874

> . . . composing a poem, the tangle of images
> And jangle of words pressing hard on you, mobbing you, may
> Compel you to choose the right moment to disengage
> And find the one word, the word of command, which makes
>   them
> Meekly fall into their ranks, and the march continues . .

C. DAY LEWIS: *An Italian Visit*, 1953

Every work of enduring literature is not so much a triumph of language as a victory over language; a sudden injection of life-giving perceptions into a vocabulary that is, but for the energy of the creative writer, perpetually on the verge of exhaustion.

J. MIDDLETON MURRY: *The Problem of Style*, 1922

> . . . Trying to learn to use words, and every attempt
> Is a wholly new start, and a different kind of failure,
> Because one has only learnt to get the better of words
> For the thing one no longer has to say, or the way in which
> One is no longer disposed to say it. And so each venture
> Is a new beginning, a raid on the inarticulate
> With shabby equipment always deteriorating
> In the general mess of imprecision of feeling,
> Undisciplined squads of emotion.

T. S. ELIOT: *East Coker*, 1940

. . . words that spring from experience, and are not due to verbal habits, to the desire to be effective, to factitious excogitation, to imita-tion, to irrelevant contrivances, or to any other of the failings which prevent most people from writing poetry. . . .

I. A. RICHARDS: *Science and Poetry*, 1935

They [Shakespeare's words] are struck out at a heat, on the spur of the occasion, and have all the truth and vividness which arise from an actual impression of the objects.

WILLIAM HAZLITT

Words must be renewed, brought again into that magical and total contact with things, which they lose by use. This is what the Elizabethans did; it is what Wordsworth did, when the eighteenth century had worn away the heritage of the Elizabethans; and it is what the modern poets are trying to do, now that the nineteenth century has worn away the heritage of Wordsworth.

HUGH SYKES DAVIES: Broadcast talk on
Modern Poetry, August 1933

The bad poet dwells partly in a world of objects and partly in a world of words, and he never can get them to fit.

T. S. ELIOT: 'Swinburne as a Poet',
The Sacred Wood, 1920

His [a poet's] power of making words express what he feels is indistinguishable from his awareness of what he feels. . . . He is a poet because his interest in his experience is not separable from his interest in words; because, that is, of his habit of seeking by the evocative use of words to sharpen his awareness of his ways of feeling, so making these communicable.

F. R. LEAVIS: New Bearings in English Poetry, 1932

It is a common error to suppose that the poet differs from others only in his power over words—that we all have identical experiences but are incapable of expressing them so well. This is not so. We may have similar experiences; otherwise the poet's work would be meaningless to us. We may even have deeper experiences. But that is quite different from saying that our experiences are identical. For a poet's power over words is part of his life, part of his experience. He can never separate himself from words, any more than a painter can separate himself from colour.

The story is told of one artist—I think it was Rembrandt—who went to visit a dying friend. Afterwards he confessed that he could not sympathize completely with his friend because he was considering

the texture of his flesh, the effect of light and shade and death upon it.
So with the poet. His perceptions and sympathies are never quite
divorced from the words which might be used to express them.
Therefore we cannot say that we have felt the same experience that
the poet felt: if we had, we would have written the poem ourselves.

CLIVE SANSOM from a discarded essay

❧ WORD-ASSOCIATIONS ❧

. . . these lovely ancestral words, embalming
the souls of many common men.
OWEN BARFIELD

Words have two main functions. Firstly, they convey a meaning—a meaning which may be found in the dictionary, and is open to all. Secondly, they embody a whole world of association which has gradually grown up around them, and which derives partly from group experience (this is common to all members of the group) and partly from individual experience, which varies as between individuals, and is private to the individual.

For example, the word *cold* has a dictionary meaning which we all know. It has also a power of suggestion born of its entailed associations, some which is common to humanity, some which varies as between individuals. For myself the word carries associations, amongst others, with discomfort (a group experience) unkindness (probably a sub-group experience shared by those familiar with Shakespeare), the touch of bicycle handlebars which have no handgrips, the reflection of stone floors in unheated halls (both individual and therefore private associations), like in general but differing in the particular.

When each of us hears this word spoken, whilst we can say that in general we understand the same meaning, we cannot say we understand *exactly* the same in particular, since the impression of this word on our consciousness will have called up associations which, in so far as they are born of different individual experience, diverge. And can we doubt that there is an even more marked divergence in the impressions created in the minds of two hearers—one, say, born and bred in Singapore and the other in Archangel?

ALAN ROOK in *The Poetry Review*

. . . even the most original poet is obliged to work with words, and words, unlike marble or pigment, or vibrations in the air, owe their very substance ('meaning') to the generations of human beings who have previously used them. No poet, therefore, can be the creator of all the meaning in his poem.

OWEN BARFIELD: *Poetic Diction*, 1928

Great poetry is the fullest use of language, the use of words for the sake of as many of their associations as possible. Scientific prose tries to limit the meaning of a word to one clear, unambiguous reference; poetry tries to make use of the unlimited and often ambiguous meaning of a word. We respond to poetry not only with our intelligence, not only with our emotions, but with the whole of us.

ALEC KING and MARTIN KETLEY:
The Control of Language, 1939

In poetry, each word reverberates like the note of a well-tuned lyre, and always leaves behind it a multitude of vibrations.

JOUBERT: *Pensées*

This importance of associations is one of the principal differences between prose and poetry; I am not sure that it is not more important even than the use of metrical pattern.

MARJORIE BOULTON: *The Anatomy of Poetry*, 1953

In nearly all poetry the sound and feel of the words, what is often called the *form* of a poem in opposition to its *content*, get to work first, and the senses in which the words are later more explicitly taken are subtly influenced by this fact.

Most words are ambiguous as regards their plain sense, especially in poetry. We can take them as we please in a variety of senses. The senses we are pleased to choose are those which most suit the impulses already stirring and giving form to the verse. Thus the form often seems an inexplicable premonition of a meaning which we have not yet grasped. The same thing can be noticed in conversation. Not the strict logical sense of what is said, but the tone of voice and the occasion are the primary factors by which we interpret. . . .

In its use of words most poetry is the reverse of science. Very definite thoughts do occur, but not because the words are so chosen as logically to bar all possibilities but one. They are not: but the manner, the tone of voice, the cadence and the rhythm play upon our interests and make *them* pick out from among an indefinite number of possibilities the precise particular thoughts which they need.

I. A. RICHARDS: *Science and Poetry*, 1935

It was at Dr Richards' suggestion that William Empson wrote his famous—or, as some think, notorious—treatise on the geology of words,[1] where the main strata of associations are laid bare and Scrutinized. I can no longer recall how the seven types are classified: in fact memory seems to recall that there were seventy times seven. But I do know that the book is one that everybody concerned with poetry ought to read—as Oscar Wilde was invited to house-parties—once.

An eminent surgeon said that anatomy should be studied and forgotten—meaning, I suppose, that the surgeon's work should become instinctive. The same, I think, is true of word-anatomy. It is good to be reminded of the nerves and tissues surrounding even the simplest of words. It may persuade us, in this scientific age, that poetry needs to be read in a different way from scientific prose where 'one word, one meaning' is essential to understanding. But this knowledge must become instinctive. Imagination should be allowed to operate without Reason, the assistant-surgeon, questioning every move. Otherwise, as with so much twentieth-century verse, the patient may die under the knife.

[1] *Seven Types of Ambiguity.*

❧ MEMORY ❧

O angel Memory that can
Double the joys of faithless Man!
WALTER DE LA MARE

. . . memory is the root of creative genius. It enables the poet to connect the immediate moment of perception which is called 'inspiration'
with past moments in which he has received like impressions. This
relating of the immediate impressions with past ones enables the poet,
through the moment, to strike a kind of chord across time. . . .

The quality of a poet's memory, and the way in which he uses it,
are what chiefly distinguishes him from other poets. There are two
main categories of memory: one is what might be called overt and
conscious memory, the other is hidden and unconscious. Overt and
conscious memory is memory of impressions which at the time of their
being experienced have been formulated in the mind as ideas. Hidden
and unconscious memory is memory of impressions which have not
been consciously formulated when they were experienced, so that
remembering is like creating them anew, or like experiencing them for
the first time.   STEPHEN SPENDER: *World within World*, 1951

If the art of concentrating in a particular way is the discipline necessary
for poetry to reveal itself, memory exercised in a particular way is the
natural gift of poetic genius. The poet, above all else, is a person who
never forgets certain sense-impressions which he has experienced and
which he can re-live again and again as though with all their original
freshness. . . . It is perhaps true to say that memory is the faculty of
poetry, because the imagination itself is an exercise of memory. There
is nothing we imagine which we do not already know. And our
ability to imagine is our ability to remember what we have already
once experienced, and to apply it to some different situation. Thus the
great poets are those with memories so great that they extend beyond
their strongest experiences to their minute observations of people and
things far outside their own self-centredness.

STEPHEN SPENDER: *The Making of a Poem*, 1955

Poets are distinguished from other men ... by the greater richness and
associative power of their subconscious memories.

I. A. RICHARDS

The imagination is fed by the memory which groups together allied
experiences in such a way that one memory recalls another of the same
kind, and any experience in the present is charged with the emotion of
similar experiences in the past. ...

DAVID CAMPBELL in The Bulletin, Sydney, 14 May 1952

It is the memories themselves that matter. Only when they have
turned to blood within us, to glance and gesture, nameless and no
longer to be distinguished from ourselves—only then can it happen that
in a most rare hour the first word of a poem arises in their midst and
goes forth from them.

R. M. RILKE: The Notebook of Malte Laurids Brigge

P

❧ IMAGERY[1] ❧

*. . . the images of memory flowing in on the impulses
of immediate impression.*

S. T. COLERIDGE, *Anima Poetæ*

Imaging is, in itself, the very height and life of poetry.

JOHN DRYDEN

The human mind is not, as philosophers would have you think, a debating hall, but a picture gallery.

MACNEILE DIXON: The Gifford Lectures, 1935–7

He [Shelley] could throw a veil over his eyes, and find himself in a *camera obscura*, where all the features of a scene were reproduced in a form more pure and perfect than they had been originally presented to his external senses.

THOMAS MEDWIN: *Life of P. B. Shelley,* 1913

Under the influence of a powerful mood and its concentration, the artist is like a diver who has plunged into the deep seas of his mind. And just because he is passing down to the lower deeps his ideas are more numerous; he has a greater range of memories to tap.

ROSAMOND HARDING: *An Anatomy of Inspiration,* 1948

The vivid visual imagery . . . that suddenly distracts the inward eye on that nebulous border between waking and sleeping, appears to differ from our workaday visualizations only in the fact that it comes unbidden and unsought, and may have a perceptible relation to any context—although this may sometimes apply to the latter also. If in this state of partially-suspended consciousness we keep watch on what

[1] See also 'Metaphor', page 100.

we see, we may be astonished not only at its rapidity and unexpected-
ness, but at its beauty and variety.

> WALTER DE LA MARE: 'Dream and Imagination',
> *Behold This Dreamer*, 1939

He is pre-eminently accessible to external influences and discriminating
with regard to them. He is distinguished further by the freedom in
which all these impressions are held in suspension, and by the ease with
which they form new relations between themselves.

> I. A. RICHARDS: *Principles of Literary Criticism*, 1924

'Sensuous' for Milton, meant something like sense-perception, immediate knowledge coming to the mind without reflection or calculation,
striking direct on the mind in the same way as objects of sight or
hearing.

> W. P. KER: *Form and Style in Poetry*, 1929

. . . Sensuousness insures that framework of objectivity, that definite-
ness and articulation of imagery, and that modification of the images
themselves, without which poetry becomes flattened into mere didac-
tics of practice, or evaporated into a hazy, unthoughtful day-dreaming.

> S. T. COLERIDGE: Lectures on Poetry, 1818

It is essential to poetry that it . . . be sensuous and by its imagery elicit
truth at a flash.

> S. T. COLERIDGE: *The same*

. . . gift of the imagination in which it owns peculiarly its kinship with
the wizardry of dreams—the gift through which, on the most arid
hint, vivid ocular images spring, as in sleep, into magical clearness.

> JOHN LIVINGSTON LOWES: *The Road to Xanadu*, 1930

Almost anyone is *capable* of a vivid use of language without even
noticing it, not only in the metaphors and similes they have accepted
on trust from their parents and grandparents, but in expressions of their
own coining. A taxi-driver once told me how difficult it was driving
in the black-out during the war, with masked headlights. 'And if

someone lit a cigarette in the back of the cab,' he said, 'it was all Chinese lanterns and candle festivities.'

CHRISTOPHER FRY: 'Poetry and the Theatre', *Adam*, 1951

Images, however beautiful, though faithfully copied from nature, and as accurately represented in words, do not in themselves characterize the poet. They become proofs of original genius only as far as they are modified by a predominant passion; or by associated thoughts or images awakened by that passion; or when they have the effect of reducing multitude to unity, or succession to an instant; or lastly, when a human and intellectual life is transferred to them from the poet's own spirit.

S. T. COLERIDGE: *Biographia Literaria*, 1817

✤ SYMBOLISM ✤

Things more excellent than every image are expressed through images.
JAMBLICHUS, quoted by Emerson

In certain states of the soul, the profound significance of life is revealed completely in the spectacle, however commonplace, that is before one's eyes; it becomes the symbol of this significance.

BAUDELAIRE: quoted by J. Middleton Murry in
The Problem of Style

Poets are the first in their time to divine the darkly moving, mysterious currents, and to express them according to the limits of their capacity in more or less speaking symbols. They make known, like true prophets, the deep motions of the collective unconscious, 'the will of God' . . . which, in the course of time, must inevitably come to the surface as a general phenomenon.

CARL JUNG

. . . only a part of an author's imagery comes from his reading. It comes from the whole of his sensitive life since early childhood. Why, for all of us, out of all that we have heard, seen, felt, in a lifetime, do certain images recur, charged with emotion, rather than others? The song of one bird, the leap of one fish, at a particular place and time, the scent of one flower, an old woman on a German mountain path, six ruffians seen through an open window playing cards at night at a small French railway junction where there was a water-mill:[1] such memories may have symbolic value, but of what we cannot tell, for they come to represent the depths of feeling into which we cannot peer.

T. S. ELIOT: Conclusion to *The Use of Poetry*, 1933

Shakespeare's characters, from Othello and Macbeth down to Dog-berry and Grave-digger, may be termed ideal realities. They are not

---

[1] Readers may enjoy trying to trace these in Mr Eliot's own poems.

the things themselves, so much as abstracts of the things, which a great mind takes into itself, and there naturalizes them to its own conception.

s. t. coleridge: 9th Lecture on Shakespeare, 1811–12

Inadequate symbolism is a common weakness of bad poetry; instead of evoking the required emotion, the writer demands it by name, but despite the obvious emotional efficacy of words like 'mournful' and 'sorrowful', deep and subtle feeling can seldom be obtained by direct methods. . . . When a word is consciously recognized as a symbol of so-and-so, its effect is diminished; many poets have ruined their effect after successful evocation by stating, in a final stanzen, their prose meaning.

Author unknown

Perhaps we should make a distinction between elucidation and interpretation. We must all gratefully accept the resolution of literal and syntactical difficulties which merely impede our reading; but we must be careful how far we carry the dissolution of symbols. Symbols, the psychologists tell us, are most effective when not rationally apprehended. The deepest effects of poetry (of any art) are not due to the understanding of a discursive argument; they are unanalysed reactions to metaphors, analogies and symbols.

herbert read in *The Listener*

Imagination is the power to place a thing in its relation to the universe —or, used indifferently it seems, to the universal; it is concerned with the earth only in so far as it can use it for symbols of beauty.

Reviewer in *The Times Literary Supplement* on
Augustus Ralli's *Poetry and Faith*

❦ UNIVERSAL AND ❦ PARTICULAR

To see a world in a grain of sand,
And heaven in a wild-flower;
To hold infinity in the palm of your hand
And eternity in an hour.
WILLIAM BLAKE

If the doors of perception were cleansed, every thing would appear to man as it is—infinite.
WILLIAM BLAKE

The smallest thing may speak to a man of the whole round world.
Author unknown

Keep tight hold on the present. Every condition, every moment even, is of infinite worth because it is the representation of all Eternity.
J. W. GOETHE: *Conversations with Eckermann,* 1823

The more one digs into oneself, the more one discovers about the souls of other men.
J. W. GOETHE

At the least touch of any sense, gates to Infinity are ready to fly open.
WILLIAM ALLINGHAM

To see the eternal through the prism of the Here and Now.
AUBREY DE SELINCOURT: *On Reading Poetry,* 1952

All high poetry is infinite; it is as the first acorn, which contained all oaks potentially.
P. B. SHELLEY

. . . that extraordinary double vision of his [Hardy] which at one and the same time rested on the most trivial detail of life and beheld it in vast emotional perspective.

C. DAY LEWIS: *The Colloquial Element in English Poetry*, 1947

It [the imaginative will] is this faculty that gets beyond ordinary trivial, partial, disconnected perceptions, and finds the solemn life of the universe astir in every moment of experience.

W. P. KER: 'William Wordsworth',
Chambers' *Cyclopaedia of Literature*

The Poet should seize the Particular; and he should, if there be anything in it, thus represent the Universal.

J. W. GOETHE: *Conversations with Eckermann*, 11 June 1825

About the best poetry, and not only the best, there floats an atmosphere of infinite suggestion. The poet speaks to us of one thing, but in this one thing there seems to lurk the secret of all. He said what he meant, but his meaning seems to beckon away beyond itself, or rather to expand into something boundless which is only focussed in it.

A. C. BRADLEY: *Oxford Lectures on Poetry*, 1909

Poetry . . . is the attempt to imagine, in terms of the transitory forms of the present in which a generation lives, the universal nature of man's being.

STEPHEN SPENDER: *Life and the Poet*, 1942

. . . the power to discern the universal in the particular, and to make the particular a symbol of the universal . . . is derived not from sensuous perception but from emotional contemplation.

J. MIDDLETON MURRY: *Problem of Style*, 1922

There is a great difference between the poet who seeks the particular for the sake of the universal, and one who seeks the universal in the particular. . . . The latter is the true method of poetry.

J. W. GOETHE

Imagination is the language of genius, the power which traverses at a single glance the whole external universe and seizes on the likenesses and images, and their combinations, which are best able to embody ideas and feelings otherwise inexpressible: so that the 'things which are unseen are known by the things which are seen'.

COVENTRY PATMORE: *Religio Poetæ*, 1893

. . . the conviction that our senses are not our only trustworthy witnesses in this world, but that nature itself resembles a veil over some further reality of which the imagination in its visionary moments seems to achieve a more direct evidence.

WALTER DE LA MARE: *Behold This Dreamer*, 1939

The instinct for Beauty makes us consider the world and its pageants as a glimpse of a *correspondence* with Heaven.

EDGAR ALLEN POE: *The Poetic Principle*

. . . the quite extraordinary sense of the mind's *very being*, in suspense, above time and space; the mind with its powers of affection and memory, and its power of reading Nature in the language of God.

HUMPHRY HOUSE, on 'Frost at Midnight' in *Coleridge*

Poetry says heaven and earth in one word.

CHRISTOPHER FRY

The source of poetry is rooted in the otherness of mental or spiritual realities; these, however, are a 'nothing' until mated with earthly shapes. Creation is thus born of a union between 'earth' and 'heaven', the material and the spiritual. Without 'shapes' the poet is speechless; he needs words, puppets of the drama, tales. . . .

G. WILSON KNIGHT: *The Wheel of Fire*, 1930

. . . The double vision which sees two worlds at once, one of material reality and another of spiritual reality. . . . Poetry's sight of these two worlds in one constitutes a process which A. C. Bradley called 'the expression through sense of something beyond sense'. . . .

Poetry is both immanent and transcendent. The poet rightly feels that poetry is within himself, his own possession and of one substance with something in his being which is unique: his poetry is his and can be no one else's. But at the same time he rightly feels that it is outside himself, and that, far from possessing it, he is its servant and must submit to the will of a force greater than himself. Between these two worlds, one personal and the other impersonal, no clear boundary can be fixed; the two worlds co-exist and co-inhere, and, at the point at which they make this exchange of being, poetry is conceived.

R. H. WARD: 'The Mind of Poetry', *The Aryan Path*

> The poet's eye, in a fine frenzy rolling,
> Doth glance from heaven to earth, from earth to heaven;
> And, as imagination bodies forth
> The forms of things unknown, the poet's pen
> Turns them to shapes, and gives to airy nothing
> A local habitation and a name.

WILLIAM SHAKESPEARE: *A Midsummer Night's Dream*

It was Shakespeare's prerogative to have the universal, which is potentially in each particular, opened out to him, the *homo generalis*, not as an abstraction from observation of a variety of men, but as the substance capable of endless modifications, of which his own personal existence was but one, and to use this one as the eye that beheld the other, and as the tongue that could convey the discovery.

S. T. COLERIDGE: Lectures on Jonson, Beaumont, etc., 1818

Even when, as in *Macbeth*, there is anger and contempt in the rejection of life, there is exaltation also; we are not cast down, but uplifted by them. It is hard to translate a feeling so mysterious into words without playing it false, but we might attempt to render our reaction to these passages of Shakespeare by saying that we feel that his rejection, even when angry and indignant, is not negative but positive; he rejects this life because he knows of something better and truer, even though the knowledge be against his will. When he has pronounced that life is a tale told by an idiot, full of sound and fury, signifying nothing, he is not left, as other men would be, naked to the cold wind of eternity. He has some secret knowledge of which he cannot be dispossessed and of which he cannot dispossess himself; he has a memory of some kind of experience beside which the actual experience of life is indeed trivial. He had been too deeply in love with life to deny it easily, and he was condemned—throughout what is called his 'tragic period'—to hover between rejection and acceptance of an experience which transcended it.

J. MIDDLETON MURRY: 'The Nature of Poetry',
Discoveries, 1922

. . . I imagine the indescribable glamour over the best poetry and over pictures or music, is due to its suggestion of that spiritual light which to the nature-mystic transfigures the world; and the poets and artists who make the suggestion have, perhaps unknown to themselves, seen some half-conscious or forgotten glow from that light. I do not mean, of course, that these geniuses do not make their chief appeal to our intellect, our imagination, our feelings; sometimes, as in tragedies, or in Beethoven or Wagner, there is a deliberate appeal to our bodily emotions, so to speak, by violence or jerks or noise, and others appeal to sentimentality or to animal passions. But the highest point seems to be reached by a touch which we cannot analyse or explain except by saying it is unearthly, or *uebermenschlich*, too deep for tears, or transcendent, or some other meaningless expression, preposterous were it not that they attempt to convey the inexpressible.

DOM JOHN CHAPMAN: *The Spiritual Letters*, 1935

Mysticism in its fully human sense (in the experience of the poet, the saint and the lover) is the sudden sense that beyond the changing appearance of Time there lies a life which does not change and is our home.

F. H. BRABANT: *Time and Eternity in Christian Thought*, 1937

INDEX : AUTHORS